7 STEPS TO AN UNBREAKABLE MINDSET

MIKE DIAMOND

BALBOA.
PRESS
A DIVISION OF HAY HOUSE

Balboa Press books may be ordered through booksellers or by contacting:

Balboa Press
A Division of Hay House
1663 Liberty Drive
Bloomington, IN 47403
www.balboapress.com
1 (877) 407-4847

Because of the dynamic nature of the Internet, any web addresses or links contained in this book may have changed since publication and may no longer be valid. The views expressed in this work are solely those of the author and do not necessarily reflect the views of the publisher, and the publisher hereby disclaims any responsibility for them.

The author of this book does not dispense medical advice or prescribe the use of any technique as a form of treatment for physical, emotional, or medical problems without the advice of a physician, either directly or indirectly. The intent of the author is only to offer information of a general nature to help you in your quest for emotional and spiritual well-being. In the event you use any of the information in this book for yourself, which is your constitutional right, the author and the publisher assume no responsibility for your actions.

Any people depicted in stock imagery provided by Getty Images are models, and such images are being used for illustrative purposes only. Certain stock imagery © Getty Images.

Print information available on the last page.

ISBN: 978-1-9822-1053-3 (sc)
ISBN: 978-1-9822-1054-0 (e)

Balboa Press rev. date: 08/17/2018

CONTENTS

CHAPTER 1: BREAKING FEAR

In life we all have a role, or as some people like to say, a *purpose*. It's our reason for why we exist. There are no guarantees in life. In my life, I've learned that absolutely nothing is for certain. No one has a crystal ball that allows them to know when their time is up. That uncertainty is what gives our life meaning. Life is a sacred gift and so is the time we spend here on Earth.

Knowing for a fact that nothing lasts forever, I often wonder why we spend so much of our precious time on things that truly have no meaning at all. As I said, *one thing is for sure, there are no sure things in life.* Living with the knowledge that there are no guarantees, I've discovered only two certainties. Ben Franklin got one of them right when he said that "nothing is certain in life, but death and taxes." Old Ben was right, death is a certainty. However, the second is equally as scary—*change.*

The ultimate reality is that we are either motivated by death, or we are paralyzed by its possibility. Unfortunately, most people are controlled by their ego, which causes us to fear death and its finality. So, the question is, what are we afraid of? And why are we afraid of it?

The unknown, no matter how much we think we can wrap our heads around it, is too much for us to deal with. We know that when it comes to death, we literally know absolutely nothing. Only until we actually experience it for ourselves will we truly know what it is like to die.

The second guarantee is that time will change us, but we still get to choose how we use it. As I'm writing this right now, I have made a choice with the time I've spent to put these words on this page. As time passes, I can't get back the time, but I can keep coming back to the computer, again and again. You see, we must make judgement calls in the face of the unknown. We can never go back in time to change our decisions, but we can learn how to keep moving forward.

We can either make the most of the time we have on this planet, or we procrastinate and waste it. Sure, life can be unfair, but like anything else, we have to make a choice to either accept the reality we are faced with day in-and-out, or to run from it.

To find our role in life we must take the time to really look at ourselves and the choices that we make. If we are not prepared to live in reality, and to understand our assets and liabilities, we will always blame the world for our problems. The easy way out is to become a victim, say life is unfair and take no responsibility and action to be successful. Unfortunately, most people would rather be lazy and look for the easy way. How many health ads do you see every day promising quick results? Sorry to say, but they don't work. Good old-fashioned cardio, lifting weights, and no carbs has always gotten me ripped. It sucks, but as Kate Moss said, "food never tastes as good as skinny feels."

We live in a quick fix Instagram, instant gratification world. We have no attention spans and we can't focus for more than ten seconds. And yet we wonder why we all have so much fear, anxiety, stress, anger and frustration in our lives. Breaking our fear is not hard, but it's going to take some work—some real work. They say it takes a minimum of sixty-six days for a discipline to become a habit. We have to create good habits and be consistent if we are to see some positive change in our lives. There is no golden goose to lay the special eggs. Jack's magic beanstalk is out of business. If you want to create a million-dollar mind set it starts with breaking your fears. If you're ready to do that then keep reading. If not, then this book probably isn't for you.

ROLE
R-Remove
O-Obstacles
L-Live
E-Empowered

We must remove obstacles to live empowered. So, what are the obstacles that stand in the way of us finding our ROLE?

Is it our age, height, weight? The color of our skin, our eyes, or our hair? Where we are born, the language we speak or don't speak?

I personally don't think it is any of these things. I believe there is one factor that rings true with anyone who succeeds in life. People that succeed in life do the work no matter how they feel, while unsuccessful people only do work when they feel good.

Why is this generally true? It's because successful people know how to manage their fears. We are faced with fear day and night no matter where we travel, or who we are with. We need to face our fears if we are going to succeed and be happy in life. Just by saying the word *fear* people start to get anxious and stressed. One thing that I always tell people is that there is no such thing as stress management, there is only *fear management.* When you can learn to manage your fear, you won't have anything to stress about.

FEAR

F-False

E-Evidence

A-Appearing

R-Real

When false evidence appears real most people…

F-Fuck

E-Everything

A-And

R-Run

But instead we must…

F-Face

E-Everything

A-And

R-Rise

Yes, as simple as it sounds, we must face our fears to rise above it all. You may say "well that's easier than it sounds."

Before I show you how to conquer your fears, let's first take a look at fear and how it affects us in our life.

FEAR MANAGEMENT

We all have different fears. Some people are afraid of mice, other people are afraid of heights. I personally hate roller coasters! I would rather take on a tiger in a fight than sit on a rollercoaster for five minutes! When our fears start to affect our lives in a negative way we have to start examining them. Being afraid to ride a rollercoaster doesn't affect my life in a negative way. It doesn't stop me from achieving my goals or going after my dreams. But for years, I had issues reading as I was yet to be diagnosed as dyslexic. I did horrible during my school years and it caused me a lot of problems in life, until I finally addressed these issues.

Not being able to understand contracts, lost me a lot of deals. I have had to work overtime to build up my reading and writing skills—even writing this book has been painstakingly difficult for me. But, I have other skills that make up for my lack of ability in certain areas. I will always carry the fear of reading out loud in public. But over the years, I have learnt to conquer this fear, day by day. Because if I didn't, I would have been able to open up businesses, build brands, and shoot TV shows.

Fear is not bad, if we use the energy it produces in a positive way. Fear won't just disappear if we ignore it. Like anything else in life, we have to work on it. Blocking it or pushing it aside does not benefit us at all.

I know a lot of people are afraid of confrontation and become non-stop people pleasers. They lose themselves, their dreams, and their goals because they are afraid if they're honest about who and what they feel, people will not like them. My whole life I was taught to put other people first and that my opinions didn't matter. I would rebel constantly and got in all kinds of trouble as a teenager. My parents were horrible people pleasers and are constantly miserable because of it. I was told I would never come to America. Yet, I have lived in America full-time since 1997. I was told I was a loser, dumb, and was destined to spend my life behind bars. (Part of that is true, I have opened up multiple world-renowned bars and restaurants, and as a result have stood behind the bar on many occasions. However, I don't think that's what my haters had in mind.

In fact, I have been clean and sober since 4/14/06 and I have helped hundreds of people to get clean. When I first attempted to get sober, people laughed at me, and said I didn't stand a chance of staying clean.

When I got thrown out of high school at sixteen for smoking and dealing pot, no one gave me a chance. But I knew deep down that wasn't my reality. Other people's opinion of you is never your reality unless you make it your reality.

If you let people rent space in your head, they will own you and destroy you. No one knows the magic that lives inside you. And no one has the right to tell you your future. If you truly believe you can achieve something, deep in your soul, and are committed and do the work, nothing can stop you, except you. If you stand in line long enough guess what? You get to the front. Too many people quit before the magic happens. The only easy day was yesterday. It's time to face our fears and rise above them.

Fight and Flight Mode

You have probably heard of fight or flight mode before. This is how you must respond to adversity in order to rise above pressure and make the most of your opportunities. To keep it simple, the easiest way to explain it is through our friends in the animal kingdom.

Animals live in *fight or flight mode* for their survival. Take a zebra for example. Imagine that he is on his lunch break eating berries near a watering hole. He senses something isn't right as there is a restless energy in the air. Little does he know that it's the lion's lunch break and he's on the menu. A lion is fast approaching about thirty feet away in the long grass, and about to enter into fight mode. The zebra will need to get his lunch to go or he's about to have a really bad day. When we sense danger, our body responds to that danger. There are many instances where people have shown super human strength to save loved ones when they go into fight or flight mode.

So now let's look at how to kick our fear in the butt. When we feel fear the first thing we have to do is STOP.

S-**Stop** what you are doing.

T-**Take** a breath.

I actually suggest taking about five to ten slow, deep breaths. If you have ever watched a boxing match or UFC fight, the coaches will always tell the fighters to breathe as soon as the round is finished. When we sense danger, our body responds accordingly to help us. We go from our rest and digest mode to fight or flight. The parasympathetic nervous system switches to our sympathetic nervous system, blood rushes to our hands and feet, and we are ready for action. The only way to control our nervous system is through deep diaphragmatic breathing. When we are in our rest and digest system we can operate out of our pre-frontal cortex where we make all our executive decisions. When we are in fight or flight mode we are operating out of our lizard brains and only reacting to the present danger. That's why we don't make good decisions when we are charged with emotions, either anger or fear. Remember to BREATHE!

O-**Observe** your Fear.

Four things are happening when you are afraid.
1. You're either afraid you're not going to get what you want.
2. Fearful you might lose what you have already got.
3. You are afraid of the future.
4. Or, you have guilt and shame for something you have done in the past.

P-**Proceed** to take actions to remove and conquer your fear.

Ok, let's take a look at the different domains of fear.

The Many Faces of Fear

Crime
1. Murder
2. Rape
3. Burglary
4. Fraud
5. Identity Theft

Daily Life
1. Romance
2. Rejection
3. Ridicule
4. Talking to strangers
5. Meeting new people

Environment
1. Global warming
2. Overpopulation
3. Pollution

Government
1. Drones
2. Healthcare
3. Immigration
4. Taxation

Judgement of Others

1. Appearance
2. Weight
3. Age
4. Race

Man Made Disasters

1. Chemical Warfare
2. Terrorism
3. Nuclear war

Natural Disasters

1. Earthquakes
2. Droughts
3. Floods
4. Hurricanes
5. Tornadoes

Personal Anxieties

1. Tight spaces
2. Public speaking
3. Vaccines
4. Heights
5. Spiders
6. Snakes

Personal and Future

1. Dying
2. Illness
3. Running out of money
4. Unemployment

Technology

1. Artificial intelligence
2. Robots
3. Cyber terrorism

Here is a list of the top fears we might have and the corresponding reason we have them.

FEAR	FEAR DOMAIN	EFFECTS
CORRUPTION	GOVERNMENT	Lose What I Have.
CYBER TERRORISM	TECHNOLOGY	Lose what I have.
TERRORIST ATTACKS	MAN MADE	Lose what I have.
IDENTITY THEFT	CRIME	Lose what I have.
ECONOMIC COLLAPSE	MAN MADE	Not get what I want, lose what I have
RUNNING OUT OF MONEY	PERSONAL	Lose what I have, not get what I want, worry about the future.
CREDIT CARD FRAUD	CRIME	Lose what I have, not get what I want, worry about the future.
GUNS	CRIME	Lose what I have meaning my life.
ILLNESS	PERSONAL	Lose what I have, the future, not get what I want.
TORNADOES	NATURAL DISASTERS	Future, lose what I have
IMMIGRANTS	GOVERNMENT	Lose what I have
DROUGHTS	NATURAL DISASTERS	Lose what I have
ROBOTS IN THE WORKPLACE	TECHNOLOGY	Lose what I have, my future, not get what I want.

EARTHQUAKES	NATURAL DISASTERS	Lose what I have, the future.
UNEMPLOYMENT	MAN MADE	Lose what I have, future, not get what I want.
DEATH	PERSONAL	Future
AGING	PERSONAL	Future
MASS SHOOTINGS	CRIME	Lose what I have, the future
THE POLICE	GOVERNMENT	Lose what I have, the future
PUBLIC SEEKING	PERSONAL	Not get what I want, the future
CHANGE	PERSONAL	Lose what I have, the future
INTIMACY	PERSONAL	Not get what I want, the future
FAILURE	PERSONAL	Not get what I want, the future
REJECTION	PERSONAL	Future
COMMITMENT	PERSONAL	What I have, not get what I want lose
SUCCESS	PERSONAL	Success, my future
FLYING	PERSONAL	Future

Go through the list above and see if any of these affect you your life goals and dreams. We are all different and are impacted differently. One fear for one person makes no sense to another. But to be truly happy and successful, we must be able to accept the reality of fear and make it our friend. We must go through our fears daily and get used to facing them.

Once we create the habit of facing our fears they no longer exist. Think of a fear you had in the past that you don't have anymore. I remember when I first started to drive a stick shift. It seemed nearly impossible when I first got in the car. Clutch, gas, gears, mirrors, indicators. It was so hard to find the sweet spot, and I would grind them until I found them. But day by day, as I practiced and really focused, it finally all flowed. Think about things you have done and how you managed to rise above your fears when you did the work.

Fear as Your Friend

To say our fear can be our friend seems insane. However, I believe there is always two sides to every coin. My upbringing was very negative and full of pain, and during that time I learned that it takes just as much time to think a positive thought as it does to think a negative thought. So honestly, why do we waste so much time being negative? It's pointless and makes absolutely no sense to cry over spilt milk and be full of fear, when nothing comes with us when we die.

My fear of not being successful, or not having enough time to make my dreams a reality has always motivated me to work hard and keep failing until I succeed. When you make a mistake it's vital that you learn from it. There is no point in playing it safe when, as Jim Morrison said, "no one gets out alive."

You can sit in your room all day and pray that you won't die and guess what—you still will. You can either accept the fear and use it to motivate you, or not, it's ultimately your choice.

Acting School

After a solid year of sobriety things were moving alone fine, or so I thought. The pressure of moving to a big city and working two jobs to pay for acting class started to take its toll on me. I always thought I could control my drinking and drug use on my own. I felt it was mind over matter. Unfortunately, I had to learn the truth the hard way.

After a non-stop week of work, rehearsals and class, I decided to go on a bender. I was rolling with a heavy crew, so things got out of hand quickly. Friday night turned into a 5-day bender of insanity.

I showed up to class wrecked and my work was beginning to suffer. One of my teachers pulled me aside and tried to talk to me, but I wouldn't have it. He would often drink and party with us, so I found his advice hypocritical, even though he was just trying to help. I wasn't in the mood to have him lecture me as I thought I had all the answers. Instead of taking his advice and getting sober, I continued to party. The day in day out grind and discipline wasn't something I could deal with. Days turned into nights and nights turned into days. Living in a fog with no clarity, bad influences, and no real mentorship I finally imploded. I snapped on one of my teachers after his nonstop criticism become too much. I don't ever regret leaving school, but I do wish I would have left on better terms and in control.

So, I decided I needed a new opportunity.

The Ticket to My Future

I knew I still wanted to move to America, and I needed to find a job—*fast*. On my way to and from acting school I would pass by a clothing store named *Politix Menswear*, in the heart of Pitts St. Mall—a bustling area in Sydney. The guys working there would always brag about how much money they made. I had become friends with the shop manager named, Dean, over the past year and I'd also become friends with a few of the other guys who worked in the shop. I had a think to myself and realized I needed to ask Dean for a job.

Admittedly, he was a little confused when I first asked him for a job. For the past year every word that came out of my mouth involved two words: *America* and *acting*. I was always talking about how I was

15

going to America and how I would be an actor on TV one day. When I arrived at the store, I offered my services for a week for free right away, so he could try me out. Dean didn't take me seriously and he laughed at me with the other salesmen all standing around, which pissed me off. I said "what are you afraid of? What do you have to lose? I will grab everyone's lunch and coffee and you guys will have a personal slave for a week for free."

Dean could see I wasn't going down without a fight. My fear of not having the future I envisioned made me skip flight mode and head straight into fight mode. Dean continued to joke around with the other sales guys, all standing around laughing at me. Then he said "okay, tough guy, if you want to work here I will give you a chance but you don't have to waste my time or your time for a week."

"Are you ready to work now?" Most people don't like being put on the spot. The one thing I learned at acting school was that I am a great improviser. "Absolutely," I said, with butterflies running through my stomach.

"Okay, the next person that walks in the store, sell them some clothes. If you sell them some clothes you have a job. I don't need to waste a week of your time or my time." Instantly, I felt the rush of fear run through my body and I knew Dean thought I would back down, but he didn't know me, and he didn't know the drive I had to succeed. I stared him dead in the eyes and said, "no problem." I knew he thought I would fail and so did the other salesman in the shop. A moment or two later, a lady walked in off the street and started to browse around. Dean gave me a nod as if to say *do your thing*. I approached her slowly and asked her how her day was. I didn't know much about selling clothes, but I knew enough to know I wasn't selling clothes, I was selling me.

I asked a few questions to try and get an idea of what she was shopping for as it was a menswear boutique. She finally said she was looking for something for her son because it was his birthday next week. Like a shark, once I smelled blood I went in for the kill. I had too much to lose to lose this sale and a job offer. That's how my fear was motivating me to work harder. I had an idea and started to improvise. "Do you mind if I show you a couple of outfits I like?" I asked her, trying to sound as polite as possible. The lady smiled and nodded "yes." Not knowing the stock in the store, I looked at the display window and quickly put together an outfit. Then I threw my curve ball.

I told the lady to give me a second and headed back to the dressing room. Dean had a confused look on his face. I went into the changing room and came out with the outfit on. Dean and the other salesman were in shock. I had sung in bands since I was fifteen, performed on stages and modelled clothes. People don't buy clothes, they buy you. Who goes into a change room and tries on clothes for a customer? A guy who wants a job so badly he will try just about anything, a guy who wants to win, a guy who will do the work to make it happen. I came out of the changing room and the lady's eyes lit up. "I love it," she said, "show me more outfits." She ended up buying three outfits that day, and I got myself a job selling clothes.

Life was going well, after that. I was making money and planning on moving to America to pursue my acting career and other projects. Dean would constantly tell me I was insane. He said, "you don't know anyone in America so why would you take such risks?" I had been working in the shop for about 6 months when Dean made me an offer he thought was the ultimate opportunity.

He offered me an area manager's position in Sydney. Not for a second, did I want to sell clothes for the rest of my life. I could have done that in Perth. However, I have never been worried about the future. Because once I put my mind to something, nothing else matters.

In life, if you don't take risks you don't get the rewards. Studies show that 80% of people will not travel further than 10 miles from where they were born. Sure, people will go on holidays and travel, but taking a vacation to another country and moving to another are two completely different worlds. Anyone can be an armchair quarterback, but a pro athlete knows the hours spent to really succeed and be a champion.

My focus was America, no matter what I was told and how many job offers I got. I would rather die trying than be afraid to give life a shot.

One day, a lady came into the store and I did my usual song and dance. She asked why I was working in a clothing store. I was honest, and I told her I was saving my money up to move to America. She said why don't you enter the green card lottery? *What green card lottery? What the fuck was she talking about?*

The next day, she came by the shop and gave me a green card lottery ticket. I thought the lady was insane, so I went to the American Embassy and asked them if it was legit. They told me it was but said the chance of winning are slim to none. Well, like Jim Carrey said in *Dumb and Dumber,* "one in a million is still a chance." I sent in the green card ticket and had a really good feeling about it. I left my parent's address in Perth and told them to look out for any mail addressed to me from the American Embassy.

I was going no matter what but winning a green card would make life a lot easier. I contacted my parents a few times, and each time they said nothing had come.

Then one day, I received some mail at work from my family. And you guessed it! I won a green card. I asked my mother why she didn't tell me about the green card, or even mention it. All she said was that it is never going to work out for you, it looked like another one of your scams and dreams that go nowhere.

Like I said before, other people's opinion are not your reality. I was off to America and no one was going to stop me. Looking back, after I had lived in New York, I would go visit Dean from time to time, and he would still be grinding away in the shop. He never went on holidays, and he never took risks to pursue his dreams. He was always full of fear and anger and would tell me I took too many risks, and ask me when was I going to grow up, settle down, and have a family? Dean passed away a few weeks after I saw him on my last visit back home. He was fifty years old.

He was waiting to go on his big vacations when he retired, but he never got there. His fear wasn't his friend, it immobilized him. And here I am—the kid with barely any education from a small town with big dreams who has lived in Miami, NYC, LA and Las Vegas. My secret was never looking back and always looking for a challenge. I bought a one-way ticket and threw it all on the line.

Was it luck winning the green card? Was it fate? Or, was it that I faced my fears and allowed the Universe to take care of me? What would have happened if I stayed in acting school? What would have happened if I would have let Dean laugh me out of that clothing store?

Have faith and face your fears and the Universe will always give you what you need to succeed. No one will run the marathon for you. It's your race, your life, your movie. Edit out the characters you don't want. You are the star and it's your time to shine. No matter how old you are, or how young you are, don't complain about your life and the people around you. Don't wait for the world to change, because the world will stay the same. Other people will stay the same. Create the change. Be the change.

CHAPTER 2: SOLUTIONS TO SITUATIONS

We all must accept the inevitability that we will be faced with problems in life. Not all problems are created the same, they have a gradient that includes: bad situations, unpleasant situations, unfortunate situations, and simply unfavorable situations. No matter how large the issue at hand is, our reactions to our problems define us. There are two types of people in the world. People that focus on the problem (the negative) and people that focus on the solution (the positive). It is a simple choice that we can make each and every day. Unlike animals, we always have a choice on how we can change the current situation. No matter how difficult, challenging, or how stressful, we can pick the best solution—and more importantly—the right outlook. If we focus on the negative, then that's all we will see. Whereas, if we focus on the positive, we will always find a solution to our problems—even if it's not immediately right in front of us. Our ability to problem solve and adapt to our ever-changing world is always the key to our survival. If we don't get out of our comfort zones, we will always be in trouble and we will never be able to create solutions to our problems. Learning the way to do this correctly is important, and it takes practice. No one is born 100% positive out of the womb. After all, our first noise is to scream and cry! Some people never stop being babies! All joking aside, it's vital to your unbreakable mindset to learn how to shape a positive identity.

Are you the type of person who likes to blame the world when things don't go your way? Or, do you look at the lessons learned, and experience gained by facing adversity and making mistakes?

Growing up, all I knew were people with closed minds. I heard the word "no" constantly. People who were afraid to leave their comfort zone, instantly shot down any dream that I had. Honestly, I never really understood the word "no." Every time someone told me "no" I would counter by asking "why?" I was determined to turn their "no's" into a firm "yes." Then, I would read about people like Helen Keller who despite all her setbacks was able to do amazing things. I always believed if someone like her could do something so brave, then why couldn't I? When I would tell people about my dreams, I would be told that I was dumb, and that I had bad grades. But the most important part was that I didn't let that deter me from chasing after my dreams.

Depending on what you have been exposed to in life, and the way you have been brought up, how you handle stress and unfortunate situations is going to be different. Life is going to show up no matter how much you prepare for it. If you have never been exposed to stress and have always had friends and family to bail you out when things went sideways, dealing with stressful situations may break you. People can talk all day about how tough they are, but you really see a person's true character when their backs are against the wall. When people hit rock bottom they either figure out a way to survive, shine and comeback, or they simply never recover.

When I got sober, I had to open up a nightclub just sixty days into my sobriety. I was told by nearly everyone that I would relapse. I kept it pretty simple, because making things complicated is an easy way to set yourself up for failure. I told myself, if I don't drink, then I can't get drunk. If I don't do drugs, then I can't get high. I had to shape a mindset around being positive and committing to a vision. Failure was not an option for me, so I had to be vigilant about being positive, and not getting down. Getting down meant that I would try to numb the pain with drugs or alcohol. My thoughts were extremely important to me, and my positive attitude was the fuel that led me to starting the nightclub and maintaining my sobriety.

Everyone insisted that I would fail. They couldn't believe that I could say "no" to just one drink. They told me that I was working in a nightclub, and that sooner or later I was bound to fail. I knew I had no intentions of drinking or doing drugs again. Whether I was working in a nightclub, a restaurant, a gym, or if I became a school teacher—the job didn't matter to me—I knew for sure that I was done getting loaded. People, who aren't addicts, simply don't understand. It's very difficult for them to put themselves in an addict's shoes. Speaking as a former addict, all you have to worry about when you get sober is not getting high. It's really simple. This can be pretty tough, until you build up the strength to overcome and maintain sobriety. However, that's the trick, there's really no other secret to it.

From there you can build a foundation. If you can't get the first step right in any recovery program, your doomed. Similarly, if you can't get your mind right in life, you won't be able to reach your goals. It will be impossible to perform at your best, and to actually achieve your goals for the day.

A lot of people will always blame life and others for the choices they make. I know I did that unconsciously for years, but once I changed my way of thinking and took responsibility for my choices, everything in my life changed. I never relapsed and have stayed sober ever since. I learned that if we are not prepared to face our problems head on and find solutions to the situations we are in, we can never be happy, or have the freedom that we want. Here is a list of some situations where fear of the unknown can lead you to being pretty distracted. See if you can relate to any of the items on the following list.

Having your home destroyed by a:

1. Hurricane
2. Earthquake
3. Tornado
4. House fire

What can you do to prepare for these natural disasters and horrible life-threatening situations?

Some things are out of our control, like natural disasters. But if you live in Tornado Alley and then get upset when a tornado destroys your home, you may be deceiving yourself. Don't move to NYC in February and complain about the winter. Don't move to LA and tell people you hate to drive, and public transport isn't like NYC. Do a little research and planning so that you know what you are getting into. Proper, Planning, Prevents, Piss, Poor, Performance.

5. Terroism
6. Nuclear attack

We live in a crazy world with Isis and other insane people blowing things up. I lived in NYC and watched the Twin Towers come down on September 11. I dealt with the situation, but I'm not going to lie, it was extremely tough living in NYC at that time.

7. Car accident
8. Being burgled at home or a home invasion
9. Credit card fraud, identity theft
10. Being laid off
11. Getting a divorce

12. Losing a Loved One
13. Losing a Beloved Pet
14. Getting Cancer
15. Breaking Bones
16. Having Surgery

Take a look at these situations, some you may have already faced. How did you handle yourself in these situations? What can you do to prepare yourself for problems you may face in the future?

I dealt with a house fire a couple of years ago. I had great insurance and things turned out better after the home was fixed up, as it needed a little renovation, anyway. I was diagnosed with Ulcerative Colitis a few years back. The doctors put me on so many drugs I was going insane. I got so sick I was told that if my colon weren't removed I would get cancer. I began to look for a solution by studying my disease, which is incurable. Through strict dieting and a change of lifestyle and no drugs, I put myself into remission. Doctors constantly told me, that I would get cancer if I didn't have my colon removed. I just never felt that having a poo bag (even if it was made by Prada) is something I ever wanted for myself.

Another horrifying experience was when my appendix burst a few months back and I went into septic shock. The recovery was tough, but I did what the doctors told me, and I slowly recovered. It was a crazy day. I found out that I was going to be a father. My appendix burst on my birthday and I signed a lease in NYC to open a restaurant. When I was about to go into surgery things weren't looking the best. But I had faith I would be okay. I got through the surgery despite low odds, and the doctors still wanted to take out my colon, but I wouldn't let it happen. They put me on a ton of opiates, which was scary being an ex-addict. I took what I was told and when it was time to come off of them, I had no problem at all.

The point of this story, is that no matter what you are faced with you can begin by looking for solutions to life's problems and really take the time to figure out what it is that you need to do. Stop wasting the energy on the problem when instead, you can use that energy to be looking for a solution. All of the great men and women of our time were solution driven and answers focused. When faced with adversity they rose to the occasion and shut the mouths of the naysayers and haters.

CHAPTER 3:
TURNING YOUR
DREAM INTO REALITY

Hopefully, you have started to get your fears down on paper so that you can work your way up to conquering them. When you admit your fears out loud, or on paper, there is a certain trigger that goes off in your mind that allows you to realize that your fear isn't that scary.

It's kind of like saying *abracadabra*, once you expose the fear and sit with it, it's much easier to watch it disappear—just like a magic trick. The problem with fear is that it makes something that isn't real seem impossible to stop. We work it up in our heads to be much bigger than it really is. No matter what fear you are facing, you can just as easily choose to live in a way that is brave and courageous, rather than timid and afraid.

Even if you are on your deathbed, unable to beat cancer, you can still live the rest of your days in a way that makes the most of your life. Winston Churchill, for example, smoked cigars and drank whiskey with his family. Even in the direst of circumstances, you can still make the most out of the time that you have on this planet.

When I was living in New York City during the terrorist attacks on 9/11, I remember vividly the feeling of pain, fear, and sheer panic that surrounded the city. Everyone was on edge, including myself. I've been in countless fights with guys twice my size but seeing thousands of people running and screaming for their lives was more than I could have ever prepared to face.

However, later that night on the news I was amazed by the bravery and the sheer lack of fear that those firefighters and police officers had at Ground Zero. They rushed in, some of them knowing they had a slim to zero chance of coming back out alive. I'm not a crier, even if I get kicked in the nose, I'm still going to spit out blood and look to get even, but that night seeing those brave men and women got to me.

I thought about how scared they must have been. Their families and loved ones, all at home, hoping that they would make it home to them that night. And how they knew that they probably would never be able to say goodbye again, as they rushed into help complete strangers. In the face of courage there isn't any time for fear. Remember that and keep going. Your heart is much stronger than your head.

Clear the Fear

By now, you've started to see how you can begin taking some responsibility for the choices you make. You've seen how playing the victim isn't a good fit for you and the life that you want to create, and that the only way to truly overcome that fear is by facing it. You've started to problem solve by creating plans and sticking to them. No more excuses. So now, let's look at how to turn a dream into a reality.

Dreams

I truly believe you can turn any dream into a reality. What I mean by that is that if I tell you I'm going to run the 100m in 9.97 seconds I'm not living in reality. Now, I was a solid athlete when I was younger. In my prime, I was an Aussie rules rugby player and knew my way around a rugby pitch. However, my best time in my senior year of high school was 11.09 seconds. I would average around 11.5s.

You have to be honest with yourself about why you're doing what you're doing. I loved to play sports, but running wasn't my passion, nor was it my expertise. That means that it wasn't the right dream for me to have. If I wanted to work out and spend hundreds of hours to run faster, that's what I would have done. However, if you are going to truly go for a dream, you need to be passionate about it. It has to become your life. You can make all the money in the world, but if you're building a castle of lies it will come down like a house of cards. Money doesn't buy happiness. Sure, it's nice to have it, but finding your role and purpose is the only thing that will make you happy and complete. I know a lot of people that got married, had kids, and went to college to study what their parents and peers told them to do. They weren't living their dreams, and they weren't listening to their hearts. They got divorced, had midlife crises and for what? Spend your time working on your dreams, the success will follow your passion.

I hear about a lot of dreams as a professional speaker, and as someone who has worked in both the television and music industries. Everyone has a dream—or at least, I believe that everyone *should* have a dream.

Dreams root you in reality, because they make you choose what you want in life. You can't be a professional boxer if you aren't willing to take some punches. Likewise, in life you need to make decisions that will get you closer to your goals. In order to accomplish your dreams, you need to make choices that are in alignment with what you want your end result to be. So, you have a dream, what is it and why do you want to make this dream your reality?

Be honest with yourself, don't do it out of resentment, fear, or anger. For example, if you were the shortest guy in your class and were always picked on, don't go to the gym looking to get revenge. Find something that you want for yourself, and that the world needs. Sure, you can become a world-class bodybuilder at 5'3. But don't do it to prove something to your father, or to the bullies who picked on you, do it to be of service.

Once you have your dream in sight you have to set goals. A lot of people talk about goals, and they are a pretty basic way to look at life. It truly is fairly simple. The part that catches up most people is that they don't want to create a plan and stick to it. You have to do the work no matter how you feel. When someone runs a marathon they have a plan, they set goals and take actions. If they don't it's pretty much impossible to run a marathon.

Sure, there are guys like David Goggins, the incredible Navy Seal who ran 100 miles with no training. But remember he was a trained *Navy Seal*. I ran a 13-mile half marathon without training and it was *horrific*. Always have a plan and always set goals.

Goals

We all hear people talk about setting goals, and therein lies the problem. Most people only talk about setting goals without actually talking about the work that they put in to achieve them. So many people want to tell you about the new goals they have and what they are going to do. This excitement is genuinely inspiring. However, a lot of the time, these same people never get around to talking about their accomplishments, because they never finished.

Without setting goals you will never get things done. I like to set the main goal, and I keep it as my primary focus. Then, I work backwards. I had a dream of competing against the best natural athletes in the world in a men's physique contest. So, I set that as my goal.

Then, as I'll explain later on, I asked myself if anyone in my immediate circle could help me with accomplishing this goal. That very same day, I rang a friend of mine who had competed before. He told me there was a contest coming up in September. It was July and I was in good shape. I told him my goal was to compete in the over 40 natural Olympia. I had to go and physically meet him, so he could see what kind of shape I was in. We meet up and he was honest. He said you can do it, but it's going to suck. You have never competed before and you need to win two contests in September to qualify for the natural Olympia in November. I told him I could do it.

I went home and signed up. I had to have a plan and a very thorough plan if I was to take top three in the world. Keep in mind, that this wasn't a quick weight loss plan to look good on the beach. I was competing against some of the most hardcore people on the planet! I would have to give this my all.

Now, remember when I talked about fear, and how if you don't get rid of your fear you will never make it anywhere near your dreams? Well, I have a few things working against me.

I have ulcerative colitis, which is an incurable bowel disease. So, I had to have a long serious chat with my doctor about how my body would deal with the stress of competition. I told myself, that no matter what I'm taking top three in the world. No matter what or how sick I get, or how bad I feel. My doctor asked me why I wanted to do this to myself?

In reality, I was doing it *for* myself, because I knew that if I won it meant that I could literally accomplish just about anything. It also, in many ways, had nothing to do with me. My goal was bigger than just myself, I wanted to show people with bowel disease that we can overcome anything with the right mindset. I also needed to prove to myself I could compete at a world-class level. I always said I could and showed great potential as a child but made bad choices and surrounded myself with the wrong people when I was younger, which took me off course.

It was important for me to see something all the way through. As a former addict, I have walked away from things I should have completed several times in my life. While, I've dedicated myself to sobriety for a number of years, I still am always looking for ways to expand and grow. I honestly believe that all of us need to push ourselves into areas where we are a little less than comfortable.

I decided I would do my best to place in this competition. While the odds were stacked against me, I knew that I could do it. I began by writing up a diet and workout plan for myself that I knew would challenge me. I was ready to do whatever it took, and I committed. I was actually surprised by how my body was reacting to the intensity of the workouts and the new diet plan. All was going great until about two weeks until the September contest. My stomach took a turn for the worst and my ulcerative colitis came to town.

When you live with a bowel disease, it's no joke. The cramps and constant diarrhea are insane. I was using the bathroom 10 to 15 times a day—no exaggeration. Everyone in the gym thought I was insane. I kept pushing through no matter what my body threw at me. I wasn't going to quit on myself. I unfortunately had a few accidents and had to wear a diaper some days just in case I didn't make it to the bathroom in time.

If you can imagine a forty-year-old man with tattoos, a deep Australian accent, a ponytail, and a diaper on under his gym shorts working out like a bat out of hell to achieve his dreams, then you know what sheer determination looks like. I was a machine I would work out, use the bathroom, scrub my hands, and go back to the gym for another hour. Nothing could phase me. I woke up at the crack of dawn and got my first workout in, and if I maintained a fasted state until after my workouts were complete. I was on fire and living out my dreams. Once,

I decided to commit, I never looked back. I was scared beforehand about my Ulcerative Colitis, but once I started, it was off to the races.

I made it to the September show and took first in the over 40 and second place in the novice to qualify for the natural Olympia. I had another 6 weeks of hell. I barely made it, and my wife thought I was insane, but I took third against the top natural guys over 40 in the world.

I don't tell this story to brag or boast about my accomplishments, but as a way to prove to you that you can literally do just about anything you put your mind to. I just want you to be ready to wear a diaper if you have to, instead of quitting. Don't let anything stand in your way or stop you!

If you want to make your dream a reality you need to have the dream firmly placed in your mind. You have to be able to truly see it as your reality. Then, you'll need to start setting the goals and building your team to help you make that dream your reality.

When I had a dream to have some of the biggest bands in the world at some of the most popular small clubs in the world, people laughed at me. LA had the legendary Viper Room. In NYC there was a void. So, I wanted to build a venue that was a venue for the *biggest and baddest* bands in the world. I wanted to give people an experience like no other. No one ever played in small town Perth where I was born, so It was my dream to make it happen in NYC, in a more intimate space that allowed the fans and the musicians to really connect to the music. I was lucky enough to meet the singer of the band name Fuel. We became best friends and he introduced me to Scott Weiland, the lead singer of Stone Temple Pilots, and Duff Mckagan, of Guns N' Roses. I found the space, raised the money, and Snitch RockBar was created. Velvet revolver played opening night, and the rest is history.

People, Places and Things.

Once you have a plan it's important to look at the people you are surrounding yourself with. Are they part of your team helping you to reach your goals faster, or are they distracting you? If you want to make a million dollars hang out with millionaires. If you want to get fleas hang out with dogs. The people we surround ourselves with are a huge part of our success or failures. Don't be the smartest guy or girl in the room. Get a mentor or someone that can help guide you on your way. Find a partner that supports you. Life will kick your ass when you take the road less traveled to follow your dreams. Don't be with someone who is not supportive, but make sure that you don't always go it alone. You will get enough kicks in the stomach you don't need them when you come home. Look for the right partner in your corner.

Places

Just as important as the people we surround ourselves with, are the places we go, because they can really affect the choices we make. We only have so much will power. Hanging out in bars late night drinking and doing cocaine doesn't help you get up in the morning. You can have all the talent in the world but if you hang out with the wrong people or go to the wrong places eventually you will fall.

Things

What things are you doing? Are you learning new skills? Reading books about what you want to achieve? Or do you sit on social media, YouTube and TV all day wasting time? Take a simple goal like losing weight. It's simple: cut down on what you eat and exercise consistently and you will lose weight. People will say but it's so hard? Really? No, it's only hard if you have no discipline.

Your Success Plan

Any success plan has to be realistic. In order to set yourself up for success you must be able to plan ahead accordingly. If you can't see what lies ahead, how do you know you will get there? Instead of just wandering aimlessly, you must commit to a vision of success. The fear that holds us back is that we can't see far enough ahead into the future. While this is true, it is also universally true for everyone else as well. No one has a crystal ball.

We've all failed at something before due to lack of vision, consistency, or procrastination. Yet, we all have just twenty-four hours a day. The important, life-changing question we must ask ourselves is *how do you use your time?*

Mastery takes time, and in order to commit yourself to mastery you have to plan out several years in advance. Expecting to become the next greatest prodigy is a mistake. Instead, plan on the time and effort it will take to achieve your goals so that you can plan ahead and make the impossible, possible.

So how do we plan ahead? Imagine that you have a dream of becoming a professional baseball player—not an easy thing to accomplish. However, there are several stages you must reach (both short and long-term goals) in order to get to your ultimate goal. To become a professional baseball player, you will need to play baseball for roughly fifteen to twenty years, assuming you start throwing a ball and swinging a bat around the age of three years old.

First, you'll need to grow up playing in local leagues, travel leagues, and taking advantage of opportunities at your elementary and middle schools. Up to this point, it's all just for fun—unless you are playing competitive AAU baseball, which can add anywhere from fifty to one hundred games a year to your schedule.

The first milestone you'll need to reach, competitively speaking, is that you'll need to make the high school team. This will take roughly ten years of practice in order to achieve. There are roughly 500,000 high school baseball players. However, that number drops down to roughly 100,000 senior year varsity athletes, because most people quit before the end of their time in high school. After playing for four years, you'll need to play college baseball, unless you are the lucky and incredibly gifted 0.5% who are drafted to the major leagues from high school (more on that later). 25,000 College baseball players make the team their freshman year (some on scholarships, some not). However, by the time senior year rolls around in college, only about 5,000 baseball players are left. Out of that 5,000 only 600 NCAA athletes get drafted. The probability that you will get drafted is roughly 10% if you play college baseball, which by the time you graduate will have taken 20 years to reach.[1]

Even after getting drafted, you will most likely need to spend one or two additional years in the minor leagues, before getting called up to join the professional team. Also, once you get called up to the big leagues you may not make the season roster, which means more time back in the minor leagues, before getting called back up—if it happens again.

Knowing how difficult it is doesn't stop most children from dreaming about the Major Leagues. However, this is a great metaphor for what it will take to achieve absolute mastery. So instead of just writing down a few things casually, I encourage you to really think hard about what you will need to do and how long you will need to commit to each step of your journey to achieve mastery.

---

[1] http://www.hsbaseballweb.com/probability.htm

WHAT IS YOUR 10-YEAR GOAL?

WHAT IS YOUR 5-YEAR GOAL?

WHAT IS YOUR 1-YEAR GOAL?

WHAT ARE YOUR MONTHLY GOALS?

WHAT ARE YOUR WEEKLY GOALS?

WHAT ARE YOUR DAILY GOALS?

Okay, so now you have a dream and it's out on paper. That's a great start, but it's still just a start. Now, you need to commit yourself to realizing your dream and making it happen. To get started, ask a few key questions and devote yourself to finding the answers.

Do you know anyone else who has achieved what you are looking to achieve?

If so, what did they do to achieve it?

Follow these three steps:

Create a plan.

Get a mentor.

Set your goals.

Who could you surround yourself with to create your dream team?

Where are you going, and where are the places you are spending your time? If they aren't in alignment with your goal, write down where you could spend more time.

Are you walking towards your dream, or being pulled away from it?

What things are you doing daily, weekly, monthly, yearly?

Post Traumatic Growth

To be successful at anything you have to train yourself to never quit. Like the Navy Seals say, *when you think you're done, you have 40% left to give.* You must be consistent, disciplined, dedicated, enthusiastic, and honest with yourself. Each day, show up and shut up, no matter how you feel, create good habits, and die before you quit.

When I was competing in the Olympia I got so sick with my Ulcerative Colitis my wife said to me, "I think you're going to die doing this contest." I said, "honey if an 8-ball of cocaine and a bottle of vodka a day couldn't kill me, fitness won't. And if I do, please have an open casket cause I'm going to be ripped!"

We have all faced some kind of trauma in our lives. We have all heard about post-traumatic stress disorder. But how many people are able to look at it this way?

Our adversity and pain make us stronger and more resilient. So next time you're under stress or face adversity know that you will grow from the pain and stress. The trauma makes you stronger and unbreakable. We can't change people or what they do to us, but we can choose how we feel about it.

It's been said what doesn't kill us makes us stronger. The more adversity we face, the more resilient we become. Victor Frankel is the prototype for this kind of Post Traumatic Growth. In the legendary book Man's Search for Meaning, Victor takes us up close and personal by chronicling the time he spent in a concentration camp.[2] Surviving

---

[2]   Frankl, Viktor E., et al. *Man's Search for Meaning.* Beacon Press, 2017.

the worst imaginable situations, Victor programmed his mind to find gratitude in the little things and coached the other prisoners with his positivity. Victor made it out alive, yet he lost his entire family. Most people would have been destroyed with what he had experienced but Victor used his experience to create *logotherapy*: which is a type of therapy that involves pursuing your life's purpose in order to find happiness. Victor is the perfect example of what Post Traumatic growth is. We need to find gratitude in the small things, and not let one event define the rest of our life experience. It won't be easy but following in the footsteps of the great Victor Frankel and changing our perception when we are faced with adversity can open up a world of change.

CHAPTER 4: CRUSHING YOUR INNER CRITIC

Your inner critic will vary depending on what type of childhood you experienced. Specifically, your ability to self-police your inner critic will come down to what type of environment you were raised in. Just like raising a plant in an environment that helps it grow and flourish, children are very malleable. Our actions, words, and discipline mold them into the types of adults, who they will later become. Just like a potted plant, children are very fragile and must be handled with great care to ensure that they grow up strong and healthy. While many children are well nourished by their parents physically, not every child grows up in a supportive home emotionally. This is where the inner critic comes from. Not everyone's inner critic came from home— some come from schoolteachers, bullies on the playground, or other influences in our life. Sometimes an embarrassing moment can be highly traumatic for the child. No matter where this inner critic comes from, the important fact to remember is that we all have one.

Even if you were surrounded with love and encouragement, you still have doubts. These doubts are the root of the inner critic. However, if you were supported emotionally as a child, you are probably a much more confident person than many of your coworkers, friends, and colleagues.

If, on the other hand, all your life you where bullied called a *loser, dumb, fat,* or *stupid,* then you're going to have some negative thoughts running through your head. This is normal, and perfectly natural. Our inner critic is not something that we need to be ashamed about; it is just simply something we have to work around.

The biggest reason that we must learn about our inner critic and become aware of it is that if we leave it unchecked it can cause problems in our life. Once you commit to taking control of your dreams and moving forward in your life, your inner critic will decide to rear its ugly head. This is normal, but it is something that we must always be on the lookout for. By knowing that the inner critic is silently lurking around the corner, you won't be surprised when he shows up to thwart your dreams.

Inner critics can cause us a tremendous amount of pain. They want us to fail, because they are the aspects of ourselves that never received love. They are trapped in fear and want to keep us stuck there. They are afraid that if you go out and do something brave, that it will actually become a lot worse for you.

How we choose to think affects how we feel. How we feel affects how we act. Our actions become our life story, good or bad. Unfortunately, we can't choose our parents or our siblings. I know we all wish we could sometimes! And like most people in the world we all come from some sort of a dysfunctional family system.

Most families repeat cycles without ever questioning what they do, or why they do it. What we are exposed to as children affects who we are, and this has both positive and negative effects on our personalities. We get our good and bad habits from the people who we spend the most time with. If all you see is anger, violence, pain and negativity then you will begin to reflect and act that out in your life. On the other hand, if you are surrounded by joy, happiness, and positivity it is much more likely that you will grow up with encouragement and live an empowered life.

The good news is that we can remove the negative and replace it with something positive if we are prepared to do a lot of work on ourselves. Bad habits can be replaced with good habits, but it takes a lot of honest and consistent work. The thing about self-work is that it is easy to avoid, and it can be painfully hard. I've worked in tattoo shops around the world, and I've seen some pretty insane body scarification. However, the inner work that is needed to actually silence your inner critic, isn't easy, and can be painful. Why? Because it causes us to look at our shame, our shadow side, and deal with emotions, events, and circumstances that caused us pain.

Studies show that the first three years of a child's life are the most important. The information gathered during this period can affect the child for the rest of his or her life. What we choose to pass onto our children gets stored into their subconscious minds. If as parents we don't know who we are and why we think the way we think (and have not done any spiritual work on ourselves,) we will repeat cycles without even knowing it. We all have seen people in bad relationships saying how bad their parents were and doing the exact same thing that they did. These people aren't self-aware enough to recognize that they are repeating the exact same cycle over and over again. If we don't take responsibility for our actions, and instead, always blame the world and our families for the choices we make, we can never make a positive change.

The times have changed dramatically since I was a child. When I went to school, teachers had no problem giving us the cane for punishment. If you were bullied by other students, you were bullied, plain and simple. The beatings I took from fellow students, my teachers, and my parents were nonstop. I could barely read because of my debilitating dyslexia, which no one was able to diagnose from the outside.

When I was in second grade, my teacher would call me up in front of the class every Tuesday to read out loud while the other kids laughed at me. For some reason my teacher thought my reading would improve. It did the opposite, it just made me regress. I was too afraid and embarrassed to ask for help. Instead, I felt resentment, anger, and I really wanted to get revenge.

It has taken a lot of hard work to improve my reading, writing and spelling. In today's world, a teacher might be fired if a parent felt their child was being singled out, or intentionally being made fun of for a learning disability. If a teacher lays a hand on a student now, it becomes a viral video and there is hell to pay. I'm glad teachers can't hit kids like they used to. However, I do feel that we need better parenting at home and that starts by having parents who are self-aware of themselves, and who can encourage their children to do what is right and correctly discipline them when they are acting out.

Constructive and Non-Constructive Criticism

If you were lucky enough to have positive parents, teachers and coaches who believed in helping you reach your goals you received what's known as *constructive criticism*. We all need helpful suggestions to create positive change in our lives and improve. Good role models and mentors can help guide us through life's problems. When someone knows how to be constructive in their criticism they can give the right suggestions to help someone grow and improve in what they are doing. Even though it might be negative, it doesn't come off negative, if done correctly.

If someone makes a mistake, yelling at them and shaming them doesn't improve their confidence and self-esteem. Instead, this creates a bigger problem. One of the problems that we have created in our society is that we shame people for doing things that are bad, or for being wrong. Instead of correcting the mistake and making changes to the behavior, we yell, scold, or belittle people. There's a very important distinction that needs to be made, and this is where most people get it wrong. People are not bad people for doing something wrong—they simply did something that wasn't correct. They shouldn't be demonized as individuals for who they are, instead they should be encouraged to do what is correct. Some mistakes may need a sharp correction on the leash, just like a dog who is rushing a neighbor and growling ferociously. Children shouldn't be allowed to hurt, belittle, or abuse others. However, even adults blow up in fits of rage when something goes wrong, instead of handling the situation like a calm, rational adult.

Mistakes are meant to be made, that's the fastest way to learn. When we make a mistake, *we aren't* the mistake. A good leader or mentor will offer suggestions to help you solve problems, not belittle and shame you and focus on the negative. We have all had our fair share of *destructive* criticism and critics. People who have nothing better to do, but to bring people down only cause frustration because they don't live with purpose and they aren't following their own dreams.

Think about it, if you stay in your own lane, focus on your purpose, set your goals, surround yourself with the right people who want to help you—you don't have time to be negative and talk shit about other people. The amount of hate, violence, and racism on social media and in the world today is completely insane. If you can't build someone up and be of service and positive, then why bother? If we spend more time focusing on our dreams and team building instead of being jealous and resentful we wouldn't have the issues we have today. We have to be part of the change, and we have to remember that no matter what other human beings say or do, we are the only person we can control.

Your Inner Critic

To recap, the first step that we need to acknowledge is that our inner critic is an internal voice, which was created early in life from painful experiences we have witnessed. The older we get, the more these negative thoughts become part of our reality, making it hard for us to be positive and optimistic. Imagine that you are carrying two big, heavy bags of groceries and it's not that bad at first. However, the longer you carry them the more tired you will get. You get angry, because you know you can't drop them, and you begin blaming other people, the traffic, and just about everything else. The longer you carry your inner critic around with you, the harder it is to get rid of. If we don't become aware of our inner critic, it can affect our attitude and behavior and can lead us to being self-destructive and destructive to the people around us. Our inner critic will sabotage our relationships and destroy are dreams without blinking an eye. So where does this little voice come from?

My inner critic is an interesting mix. For me, it's made up of my parents, teachers, and peers. For years in my early adulthood, I would try to overachieve to prove people wrong and win their approval, and when I didn't get the approval I thought I was worthy of, I would act out. Usually, I chose the most self-destructive means possible, which were ironically the most fun. I used sex, drugs or violence just to prove a point. My inner critic is a total prick and it will show up any time, day or night, uninvited.

"You will never be good enough." "You're a show off. You're dumb. You're ugly. You will never amount to anything! Why do you even bother? You will never make it big at anything. You will end up in jail. You're such a loser. You can't even read. You're such an idiot.

These are a few of the voices that went around my head for years. These voices mainly came from ideas I'd picked up from my good old parents and peers. However, tucked in with my inner critic was actually something pretty cool—a lesson, which taught me how to be my best self.

How to Concur Your Inner Critic

Okay, so my inner critic wreaked some havoc and chaos in my life, until I learned how to shut him down. Because for the longest time, I had to silence my inner critic by doing something crazy. Every time my inner critic got me to start doubting myself, I always began to try to prove him wrong by going crazy—*oh yeah, would a stupid person be able to...*" and off I would go into the night to get messed up, or do something stupid. It was insanity. But then, through trial and error, I began to see a pattern. This self-destructive pattern helped me see the pain that I was hiding from. And then, it pointed the way to find something better.

Then first thing to do when you recognize that you are doubting yourself because you've started listening to your inner critic is to learn how to separate your true self from your inner critic. We have to identify the internal negative voices and work out why they are there, before we can get rid of them.

It's important to be honest with ourselves and to confront our inner critic, head on. Our inner critic brings us nothing but pain and destroys our lives—*not to mention he is full of shit*. Unfortunately, the people that are part of our inner critic are also just as full of shit. From this day forward, you must focus on replacing the negative with the positive and reality of who you really are, which is amazing, smart, passionate, and full of purpose and drive.

Here is a simple technique you can use to help defeat the inner critic once and for all.

Once your inner critic is about to bash you when you make a mistake (because that's when he usually likes to talk shit) simply stop and become aware of the voice.

Ask yourself who the voice is and why it is there?

Then, write down the negative inner criticism and take a look at it.

What thoughts or feelings come up when you read the words you wrote down?

For years, I was told I couldn't sing, but that wasn't the truth. My mother told me constantly that I couldn't sing. When I started taking singing lessons, my mother even called my singing teacher and asked the teacher why she was wasting her time with me. Even when I recorded my first album my mother asked me who was singing on the record. I told her it was me. Her response? *It can't be you, because* **you can't sing**.

This is the same lady that would shame me when I won medals in track and field and even when I broke records. I was called a bloody show off. All my life I would feel ashamed when I achieved things and would sabotage myself. I started to challenge my critic and realized my mother was out of her mind. My Dad would tell me I was dumb as rocks and that the best I could do was to shovel shit into cherry bottles. Today, that's pretty funny considering I have travelled the world, opened up several world-famous bars, and started restaurants with some of the biggest rock stars in the world. I've even starred in, directed, and produced TV shows. My parents were completely wrong about me, and so anything that came from my parents had to go.

A Conscious Change Exercise

Any negative voices must be challenged and brought to the surface and exposed for what they really are: bullshit.

For example:

What I'm hearing myself say: *I am an idiot, I am dumb, stupid, and my dreams are just a waste of time.*

Inner Critic: My Father.

Is the statement true or false?

Answer: The statement is completely false.

What is the truth?

The truth is I'm dyslexic and sometimes have trouble with reading and comprehension.

What can I do to help myself?

I constantly read and write to improve my skills.

What is an asset to being dyslexic?

Being dyslexic actually works in my favor, as an entrepreneur it allows be to be creative and think out-of-the-box.

- Make a list of all the inner critic voices and work out where they come from.
- Once you do that look at whether they are true or false.
- Then, replace the negative voice with something more honest.
- Look at things you can do to improve yourself.

Just telling yourself to be positive won't work if you don't know where the voice comes from. Like any bully, once confronted, the inner critic isn't as bad as we make them out to be. Don't be bullied by your inner critic. It's time for you to make a stand and stand up for yourself. Don't be disheartened when you first start. The good news is the inner critic can be reprogrammed. Just like a computer. We have to create and install a virus remover to remove all of the negative self-talk stored in our subconscious minds.

Enter the Gym of Your Mind: Your Most Important Muscle

The subconscious mind is incredible and can be reprogrammed through autosuggestion. Like any muscle, the mind must be worked out in order to stay fit and healthy. The people who are able to become famous and achieve greatness all exercise their minds along with their physical bodies. I know that when I say this to groups during speaking engagements, a lot of people roll their eyes. They believe in having a positive attitude, but they don't really believe that it can change their life. This is true of most people, because we are not taught that our mindset has much effect on the way things work out for us in the real world. The reason they doubt this is because they don't have any proof.

There was a study a few years back with a group of students participating in a University of Chicago study led by Dr. Blaslatto in 1996. It seems like Michael Jordan wasn't the only important thing that happened to American basketball in the nineties. The reason that this study, in particular, is so vital to understanding how the mind works, is because it deals almost exclusively with the imagination.

It's pretty easy to feel good imagining what it would feel like winning the lottery, but did you know that your brain has a really tough time telling fantasy apart from reality? You may not realize it, but any time you flinch when the bad guy throws a punch on screen, or cry when Old Yeller gets shot—your brain has convinced you that fantasy is reality. Instead of using all of this mental mindset stuff to psyche ourselves out, it's imperative that we find a way to use it positively and take control of it.

Now, I'm not a yogi, and I don't believe in fairy tales. However, I do believe in the power of visualization, and that's largely because of our good friend Dr. Blaslatto. You see, his study at the University of Chicago taught us that the power of the mind to believe in something, is actually just as powerful as doing it in real life. Again, I totally know how weird and wonky this sounds. But if a 5-foot-8 dyslexic guy from Australia, with no training and a bag of adult diapers was able to place in the Mr. Olympia contest using the power of his mind, I'm pretty sure that those of you reading this book can put your minds to even better use. Because the scary fact of the matter is *our minds create.*

Thirty students in the University of Chicago study were broken in to three groups. They were all taken to the gym and were asked to shoot some free throw shots. An average was taken from all three of the groups, then they were told that they would be given special training in order to become better at making free throws.

The first group had to come to the gym every day for 30 minutes and practice shooting free throws. Each day, they went to the gym, picked up a ball, and kept a tally of how many they made or missed. They built up their arm muscles and got better at shooting free throws.

The second group was told to do absolutely nothing. They just waited around until the study concluded, and then they were called to come back in and retest. This is a way to make sure the scientific method is working. If I were in the study, back during my school days, you can bet your ass I'd be in this group—because I hated taking tests—even physical ones.

The third group was told to come into the gym and visualize through their five senses what it felt like to shoot the free throws. All they had to do was lie on the ground and close their eyes and imagine what it felt like, what it sounded like, and what it looked like to make the free throws.

After 4 weeks they brought the three groups back in to the gym to retest. The first group that practiced every day improved by 24%. The second group that did nothing didn't show any improvement whatsoever, *go figure.* The third group that did the visualization exercise improved 23% as well, which is almost the exact same amount as the group that shot the free throws for three hours per day.[3]

If we truly believe something deep in our being it becomes part of our reality. If you are able to hit a three-pointer 9 out of 10 times, but I start telling you that your form is messed up and you need to correct your elbow angle, and you'll never be able to hit that many consistently if you keep shooting that way—you may begin to question yourself. In your doubt, you will actually start to miss more free throws, because you don't believe in yourself. And your mind will start playing tricks on you to support this new doubt.

How many times has someone convinced you to do something you didn't want to do, or that you knew you shouldn't do? Then when you end up doing it, you regret what you did and begin feeling guilty. If we reprogram our inner critic, we in turn reprogram our subconscious minds. Remember how we choose to think affects how we feel.

How we feel affects how we act, and our action becomes our life story. One of the biggest things that we have to take control over are our emotions and our thoughts, because they control so much of our lives. Think about it like this, anytime you feel a certain way it influences the way that you behave. And anytime you do something, it changes the way you feel. Don't believe me?

Anytime you are sluggish, tired, lethargic—or as my dad would call it—flat out lazy, it means that you don't feel too well. However, as soon as you get up off the couch and start doing something with your day, as if by magic, you notice that your mood changes. Suddenly, your productive, you feel more positive, your outlook is brighter, and the day isn't half bad. However, it took *action* to make you feel better. Did

[3]   Haefner, Joe. "Mental Rehearsal & Visualization: The Secret to Improving Your Game Without Touching a Basketball!" *Welcome to BREAKTHROUGH BASKETBALL*, www.breakthroughbasketball.com/mental/visualization.html.

you notice that? How you think affects how you feel and how you feel affects how you act. And the combination between all three of these determines the quality and the outcome of your life.

When your thoughts, actions, and feelings are all in alignment the sky is the limit. You can create anything, because you are acting within your momentum.

CHAPTER 5:
WILL AND SKILL

There's a huge difference between those who have skill and those who have will. Most of the time, it's the people with the *will to succeed* who are able to go beyond those with sheer talent alone. Talent will get you pretty far in life; I'd have to admit that some of the most talented people I've ever met were the ones with the most success. But it won't take you the extra two-tenths of a mile you need to sprint passed the finish line in order to win. That's the job of the *will*.

Persistence, tenacity, determination—all of these words have been used to describe the will. The will is what keeps us hungry and willing to move forward, and to fight our way to the top no matter what. Throughout this chapter, I will be sharing the stories of some tremendously gifted people who were able to persevere and win despite not being as talented as the other people in their field.

Already in this book we've covered the secret to stopping fear dead in its tracks. We've worked out how to empower yourself and turn your problems into solutions. We've also gone over ways that you can enhance your ability to defeat your inner critic. Now, it's time to learn about intention.

Intentional Training

Intention means that you are doing things with the belief and expectation that they will be done. You may not get *exactly* what you want *in the way that you want it,* but you are taking action and that's where your power comes from.

All day long we work at our jobs, in our chosen profession. Some of us are trying to advance our careers, others of us are trying to moonlight as something else while we have a steady paycheck. Regardless, it's important that we make the most of our time, effort, and resources.

I believe we need to have the mindset that we are training daily to get better. Ask any Navy Seal, they don't just workout—they train. What's the difference?

Going through actions is important. You need to get daily practice in. However, practice alone doesn't make you Michael Jordan—perfect practice does. Each time you train it must be training with the intent to be world class, elite, and unstoppable. Unbreakable competitors have the utmost dedication to honing their craft and skills. This is what allows them to constantly train themselves to break down barriers and make the most of their abilities. The best in the world are dedicated to being a student of life, knowing that there are no guarantees, but making the most of their opportunities. Each day we are alive and breathing on planet Earth, is another day to improve.

We must be trained and ready to go at any time, knowing that we have acquired the appropriate skills from countess hours of pushing ourselves to our limits. When you are prepared and ready, success is imminent.

Like I've said before, we have a choice to think a certain way, which in turn, affects how we feel. Creating a million-dollar mindset is a personal choice. No one is forcing you to do this deep internal work. However, it's in your best interest for yourself to do so.

We choose to break our fears, create solutions to situations, make our dreams a reality, and conquer our inner critics not because other people want us to, but because it's what we have to do to make ourselves the best we can be. To continue on our million-dollar mindset journey we must have will and learn a certain amount of skills in order to be successful at anything.

Any Olympic athlete will tell you that they aren't done learning. Instead, they are lifelong students of their disciplines, because they know that they will have to constantly be improving. They are always honing their skills to get better. No matter how much talent the Universe blesses you with, it means nothing if you are not prepared to work on your skills.

This is the mistake that a lot of young athletes, students, and even relationship partners make early on in their approaches to the game of life. They believe that having the skill to do something, automatically makes them capable of doing it at the highest level. This is why the best football player in your middle school class probably never played for the Dallas Cowboys. Skill alone all by itself is *never enough*. Even the greatest superstars in the world practice and hone their craft every single day for hours and hours at a time. If they don't, they feel like they are falling behind.

During the next part of this chapter I want to take you behind the scenes of some of the toughest people who overcame subpar circumstances to achieve greatness. You see, it's not just what you're gifted with, it's what your made of that counts.

Find Your Guru

Anyone who wants to become great needs someone to teach him or her. In every superhero movie, the hero starts out as a young man or woman, who isn't very competent. Sometimes, they are *loser-ish* (think Kent Clark) and sometimes they are average like Peter Parker pre-spider bite. However, when you are in the conscious practice of working with someone better than you, you are going to succeed. A lot of people want to be self-taught these days. It seems like everyone is a *guru* of marketing or is the next Tony Robbins. However, you always need to make sure that the people you look up to and learn from are people who are actually experts at their crafts.

In order to get really good at something, you can't just learn the glamorous roles—you also have to be willing to job shadow the janitor. This is imperative if you want to be successful. You can't just learn to go on stage and be the star of the show, you must also learn the ropes of working in the wings. When you are really good at something, you know all of the minor details that help you to complete your work! Learning under a guru can help you to get the basics down, so that you can grow and succeed. You will also find things that you'd never think of to study, that will actually be really important. The more you work with your chosen guru the more you will uncover these secrets of the trade. However, these will always remain elusive to most people, and they might seem mysterious or strange to you at first. The more you work with your mentor, the more you will understand the connection. For example, sometimes musicians don't have a tech on hand to help them with technical problems during a show, if they can't figure it out on their own, or never learned, it could be disastrous.

Likewise, if you are an employee, sometimes the person above you will be out sick, on vacation, or have other obligations and your company may need your input on a subject you may have never encountered. Learning for mastery means taking a holistic approach to mastering the discovery of a subject and making the most of your ability to overcome challenges that arise. Learning your trade is the most important skill that you could ever learn to master.

However, first you must find a Guru, that's where the real work begins. We all start at the beginning. No martial arts student becomes a black belt overnight. Similarly, no carpenter learns to perfect their trade in a few weeks. Learning involves a lot of intentional training that takes precise skillsets to master and perfect. Carpenters must cut and shape wood, plastic, fiberglass, or drywall using hand and power tools.

Why Were They Greats So Great?

Every profession has their tools, and every craft has its skills. The greats are renowned for their abilities because of the time they put in to master their chops. No one is born instantly great, all of us must work at what we want.

We all know about Mozart and his music—it is the stuff of legend. But what people don't know is that Mozart started his trade at two years old.

His father was a piano teacher and had him playing non-stop, teaching him his trade. Likewise, between 1440 and 1490 Florence produced some of the greatest painters, sculptures and artists of all time. Florence was the epicenter for the social movement called craft guilds. Guilds were built on the apprenticeship system where boys from the age of 5 to 7 years old were sent to live with masters for fixed terms of 5 to 10 years. The apprentice worked directly under his Guru who assumed the rights of the child from his parents. The apprentice leaned their trades from the bottom up by mixing paints, preparing canvases, and doing menial assistant work. Apprentices spent thousands of hours under the watchful eye of their Guru honing their skills day and night, intentionally training their skills hoping that one-day they would rise to the top. Michael Angelo was working with a Guru at the age of six learning his trade as an apprentice and perfecting his skills. Knowing this, makes it easy for us to see why he and other Renaissance painters achieved such greatness.

Remember, some people are born with innate talent, and others build it by choice. Keep reading to find out how you can do the latter.

Fight or Flight

The following people are all in this chapter because they are the best at what they do, and perhaps the least physically capable of achieving it. Our whole lives we constantly compare ourselves to others. We are taught from an early age that the students who get the best grades get the most awards. The popular kids in school get all the attention, and the athletes get all of the glory and respect. The programming that goes into us as young kids tells us that we need to improve, get better, and that we will never measure up.

However, for some people that story is an outdated paradigm. The fact that they needed to "face reality" or "be more realistic" never occurred to them. In fact, it's their ability to look the facts dead in the eye and keep working hard that made them the men and women that they are today.

Some people are taught at a young age that they are never going to be good enough. I, myself, was included in this category. My parents laughed at me when I told them I had a record deal. My mom insisted that I was a bad singer. My father told me I was a lousy actor, and that I couldn't possible star on a TV show. People's opinions of you are never the honest truth—they are just reflections of their own opinions about some aspect of themselves.

If you want to know the truth, you have to look deep into the mirror and see your own eyes staring back at you to get the best answers. No one can make choices for you, and no one knows your true potential better than you.

In life we have two choices, we can face adversity and run away, or we can stand our ground, stay strong and embrace the work that it will take to get better. There's a reason nature gave us adrenaline, we can take flight, or we can stay and fight. So, let me ask you: *are you a fighter?*

Stories of Amazing People Who Weren't Skilled

David Goggins: *No* Isn't an Answer

David Goggins is the perfect example of both will and skill. Goggins has faced plenty of obstacles in his life, from dealing with asthma, sickle cell anemia, as well as psychological and physical abuse during his childhood. Goggins graduated high school with an abysmal 1.6 GPA. He was impressive by no means. But he had an even tougher roadblock standing in his way. He was obese and struggled to lose weight throughout his life.

In the late 90's, after spending years in the Air Force, Goggins who weighed close to 300 pounds was too heavy to make it through Navy Seal training. His dream was within an arm's reach, and he wasn't able to conquer it because of his physical condition. We can see already that Goggins is not a natural talent mentally or physically.

So, what does Goggins do with these handicaps? He applies the will and skill and *whatever it takes mindset* to overcome all of the obstacles standing in his way. In less than three months, he got his weight down to 190 pounds! That's an incredible feat for any regular human being. On his first two attempts to make it in through BUD/S Navy SEAL training he failed, but then on his third attempt he passed, securing the coveted rank of Navy SEAL. This training takes nearly 6 months to complete, and it involves grueling physical training that rivals the toughest workouts on the planet. Of course, there's also the dreaded hell week, which makes most people want to quit—but not Goggins.

In 2005, when he decided to run an ultra-marathon to raise money for a charity he weighted 280 pounds from years of powerlifting. He ran the marathon on his first attempt (a 100-mile race) in 24 hours. That's *all will, no skill needed!*

In May 2010, during a routine medical checkup, his doctor discovered a birth defect know as atrial septal defect (ASD), better known as a whole in your heart, this made him only able to function at 75% capacity. This condition typically prevents people from doing activities such as scuba diving or anything at high altitude. Goggins made it through Navy SEAL training, and ran ultra-marathons with little to no training, and a rare birth defect.[4] He was all will, proving that it's not always about talent—but also about making the most of the will to do well.

The Short Quarterback

Doug Flutie was by all accounts an exceptional quarterback. He was fast, could throw for completion and distance, and was one of the smartest young players in the game. However, when he sized up against NFL lineman, he was as tall standing up as they were in two-point stance. However, he could really play. And yet, many—including the coach of the Buffalo Bills, have benched him, or downplayed his success because of his lack of height.

Despite tremendous setbacks due to his size, Doug Flutie persevered. While many would have settled for a college football career, and then went into a career, Flutie chased his dreams all the way to the NFL, where he ultimately became the legend that he is today. I'm sure that there were many times that he doubted himself, didn't believe in his abilities, or thought that he wasn't going to be able to go up against larger quarterbacks. If he did, he never showed it. And his genetics were less of a factor than his sheer courage and will to succeed.

---

[4]   Chew, Louis. "David Goggins: 6 Lessons From The Toughest Man Alive." *Medium*, Augmenting Humanity, 23 Apr. 2018, medium.com/the-mission/david-goggins-6-lessons-from-the-toughest-man-alive-cb2ea26fa18.

What's Impossible?

The Doug Flutie story makes us wonder why people in our society don't believe in others. We are constantly told that our dreams are too big, and we are warned at every turn that we are destined to fail. At a young age we are taught that the *sky is the limit*, only to be told years later that we need to *be more realistic.*

People like Doug Flutie and David Goggins show us that it is not skill, genetics, or any other factor that determines our fate. Instead, it is something much deeper: the will. And this means that everything we think we know about what's possible, is false. When people say something is impossible is that really the case? We hear people all the time defying the odds and going to the extremes and pushing the boundaries. For years, experts said it was impossible to run a 4-minute mile. It simply couldn't be done. They claimed that this feat was not only humanly impossible but could kill you. The human body couldn't take the stress of running a 4-minute mile without the person's heart exploding out of their chest.

Then, Roger Bannister broke the 4-minute barrier, and the world held its breath. Would Bannister go home and die later? Would his heart suddenly burst at the seams? It didn't, as he lived until the age of 88[5].

So how did he do it? How did he make the impossible, possible? Bannister wasn't the greatest runner England had produced, yet somehow, he managed to do the impossible. An ordinary man did an extraordinary thing.

---

[5] Litsky, Frank, and Bruce Weber. "Roger Bannister, First Athlete to Break the 4-Minute Mile, Dies at 88." *The New York Times*, The New York Times, 8 June 2018, mobile.nytimes.com/2018/03/04/obituaries/roger-bannister-dead.html.

Step 1. Bannister had a goal and a vision. He totally believed he could break the mile down into four simple parts to achieve the impossible. He honed his skills and took the *macro* goal and made *micro* goals. Remember you build a wall brick by brick.

Step 2. He tuned out the outside noise. Bannister knew in his heart he could do it. He knew intuitively that it would work.

Step 3. He visualized running the 3.59-mile day and night—seeing every step of the way making it become his reality.

Step 4. He was relentless, even when he failed, he never quit on himself, knowing that it could be done if he kept grinding away.

The Iron Cowboy

As a semi-professional bodybuilder and someone who has worked out my whole life, I hate running. I would much rather be practicing martial arts, lifting weights, or boxing with someone than go for a nice long run. Which may be why I'm so inspired by the people who can literally punish their bodies by running at tremendous speeds, or great distances.

People run 100-mile ultra-marathons all the time, and yet the standard marathon is 26.2 miles. For most, running a normal marathon is impossible. For others, it's just a warm-up lap. The Iron Cowboy, also known as James Lawrence, was a regular guy who could barely do a 5k when he first started. A year later, he was doing Ironman contests.

Then, he broke a world record doing 30 Ironman contests in one year. Then, to beat his record the following year he did 50 in 50 days, in 50 different US states! That's right 50 Ironman contests in 50 days.[6] Next time you feel something deep in your soul and people say it's impossible, I want you to think about waking up every morning and running an Ironman contest, going to sleep, and doing it all again the next day for almost two months straight!

Take a step back and think for a moment about all the great inventors of our time that changed the world we live in today. If they didn't follow their callings, we wouldn't be able to do the things that we do today. It's all about mindset and how you approach a mistake. Keep grinding and don't let the opinions of others drown your voice. Remember, you never see a moving van following a hearse at a funeral. Why? Because the guy or girl in the hearse is taking nothing with them to the next life.

It's Never Too Late

One of the biggest misconceptions I see people making is that they don't believe that they can change. Or worse yet, they feel that they are too old to change their life. Nothing could be further from the truth! Remember, there is no time, time is only an illusion. If you have a dream, create the plan, set your goals and have the will and learn the skills to succeed! My life is a perfect example of lack of skill, but an abundance of will. I was nearly an old man when I took a bronze in the natural men's physique contest in 2016!

---

[6]   Sampiero, Josh. "This Cowboy Finished 50 Ironmans in 50 Days." *Red Bull*, 4 Aug. 2015, www.redbull.com/us-en/iron-cowboy-50-marathons-50-states-50-days.

I remember, when I told people as a kid that I would someday live in NYC and shoot TV shows, people laughed at me. My friends, family, and teachers all thought I was absolutely mental. I was dyslexic and a poor student, and yet I went to acting school, was willing to learn and I pushed past my barriers no matter what. In 1999 I was in a sitcom on CBS, I shot pilots for VH1, appeared on Miami Ink, NY Ink, and I even wrote, directed, and starred in Bondi Ink. When I pitched Bondi Ink it took more than a year before someone picked us up, and even then, they told me that it couldn't be done. It's so vital to your success that you stop listening to other people's opinions about you!

Remember it's never too late to shine if you have the will and learn the skills. So many people give up before the magic happens. I have always wondered the obvious question, why?

Why is it that some people give up on their dreams know nothing comes with us in the end?

Win, lose, or draw we come into the world naked and leave the world naked. It's better to have tried and failed than to have not tried at all. The train of life is always moving, you either get on the ride of your life or you miss it and sit at the station and watch it pass you by. The next time you think of throwing in the towel and thinking it is too late to shine think of these people. All will and zero skill. The reason most people miss the train is because they believe it takes too much skill. The secret is that all they needed to do is have the will to keep going.

1. 1. Ray Kroc was over 50 years old before he bought his first McDonald's in 1961, he was barely making ends meet and went on to franchise the McDonald's name. He made a fortune.
2. 2. Sam Walton owned a small chain of discount stores but didn't open his first true Wal-Mart until he was 44 and never looked back.

3. 3. Vera Wang was first known as an accomplished figure skater and fashion editor and when she decided to get married at the age of 40 she knew she wanted to a be a designer. She commissioned her own wedding dress for $10,000 and then opened her first bridal boutique the following year.

It's never too late.

Make No Excuses: Be Like an Eagle

Eagles love the storm when clouds gather, it's the perfect weather for them. In storms, eagles get excited. They use the storm winds to lift them to a higher altitude. Once the eagle finds the eye of the storm, it uses the raging storm to lift them above the clouds. This gives the eagle the opportunity to glide, which lets it rest its wings. In the meantime, all the other birds hide in the branches and trees to avoid the storm.

Are you willing to be an eagle? Will you face the storms of life and raise yourself to greater heights? Or, will you hide until the storm passes you by?

Will you run into a burning building to save someone, or when things get heated do you run out of the kitchen? You have to be an eagle if you want to succeed in life and be happy. Don't be afraid to face the storm head on.

Life gets tough, sometimes you literally have to wear a diaper to avoid the shit storm of life. I know this firsthand. But if you can ride it out, and prove that you are tougher, you can soar like the eagle, and use the momentum to reach your peak destiny!

Your Past is your Past and it doesn't Define your Future

We all come from somewhere. And all of our experiences are subjective, meaning that we are the only ones who can truly evaluate what our experiences have been—right and wrong. These experiences affect the way we look at the world and the choices that we make in life. The choices we make in life not the stories we tell create our life story.

Why is it that some people can experience horrible setbacks and still manage to rise above it all and shine, while others who appear to have it easy, just can't seem to get their shit together?

It is because until we are faced with adversity and know how to deal with loss and pressure we never find out what our true potential is. It isn't until we are pushed to the point where we feel like quitting, that we truly discover how much we want something and how much heart we really have. It's easy to blame our parents, it's easy to blame the people that have bullied us. Our past (good or bad) doesn't define who we are and what we can achieve in the future and in our lives. I'm not saying that suffering abuse, whether it's mental or physical isn't horrible—because it is. I'm not saying that coming from poverty is easy—it's not at all. If you are willing to work non-stop and follow the right path you can shine.

When I was a kid growing up in Perth, the most isolated capital city in the world, (before the Internet was around) I had to believe deep in my soul there was more to life. Your past experiences will help you move forward and learn from the people around you and your mistakes. Unfortunately, we can't change our parents, our peers, teachers, or where we grew up. But we can create our future if we are willing to work on ourselves daily. Remember, you must sweep the floor everyday otherwise the dust builds up.

My grandmother lived to 102, and she lived alone until she was 95. I remember when I called her one day and she said her arms were sore. I asked her why? She said she had bought 2 liters of olive oil to cook for the old people at the church. I was confused how old were these people? If she was 95, *how old were they*? She said she had to walk a mile home carrying the oil. She also lived on a second floor with no elevator. I asked her why she didn't catch a taxi or bus. She said it would defeat the purpose of buying the oil on sale. I laughed, as she told me that the people she cooked for were eighty, but she had stopped counting her age twenty years ago! The lady was a true legend and that mindset says it's all. If there's a will to do something—whether you're a small kid growing up in the middle of nowhere, or an elderly lady carrying her own groceries home—there's always a way to get it done.

Don't Wait to Create

Everyone has ideas but what we choose to do with them makes all the difference. Unfortunately, most people get stuck at the starting blocks and never take the first step to get into the race. Why? Is it because we are afraid to fail? Is it because we think people will think our ideas are stupid?

All great inventions or creations had to have a starting place. That starting place is the idea. The initial spark is vital, but how many people are willing to take that spark, learn the skills required to fuel the idea, and then create the fire?

When people say something is impossible is that really the truth, or is it just because no one can see our vision? Think about Roger Barrister. No one knows what lives inside of you, and what magic you have to offer. Don't be afraid to work on your ideas. While I write this, I know one person out there will be inspired with what I have to say and that is all that matters.

Every morning think of three things that are your reason for living. Mine are that I want to Inspire, Motivate and Educate. I'm willing to work relentlessly to do that. To constantly push myself to learn new skills to better myself to help others find purpose, break their fears, and make their dreams become a reality.

Surviving a Shark Attack

Getting my arm bitten off by a shark would be enough to keep me away from even a bathtub, let alone the same waters where it happened. But it didn't stop surfer Bethany Hamilton from returning to the ocean. As a thirteen-year-old, Hamilton was bitten by a 14-foot-long tiger shark. The shark snapped her board in half and took her arm with it.

She was rushed to the hospital where she later survived the attack after nearly dying from blood loss. Not only did she make a full recovery, she was able to get back on her board. At first, she had lost a lot of her skill and needed to have special boards to compensate. However, she quickly learned how to regain her confidence as a surfer.

She didn't have as much skill as she did before, but what she lacked, she made up in will. She was absolutely determined to keep surfing and has since fulfilled her dream of becoming a pro surfer, winning a silver medal at the Billabong ASP World Junior Championship in 2009. She's also appeared on nearly every major morning talk show, and has received multiple awards for her bravery, courage, and will to keep going[7].

Barbara Arrowsmith Young

Barbara's story is pretty near and dear to my heart, considering that I grew up with dyslexia. My parents and teachers would tell me

---

[7] http://bethanyhamilton.com/profile/

that I was stupid, and that I needed to try harder. Much like me, Barbara experienced difficulties with understanding language, but she also struggled to understand how numbers worked as well. This made learning nearly impossible for her.

However, she didn't give up. Instead, she was able to earn a bachelor's degree in science studying to teach children. It took her dozens of times to read her assignments before they made sense to her, but she had the will and the desire to see it through. She worked at her studies and kept pursuing her dreams of making life better for other children with similar conditions to hers.

Eventually, she was able to become an expert and she started her own school for learning impaired students called the Arrowsmith School. Her students were able to use techniques that she discovered in order to improve their learning.[8] Instead of giving up, settling, and deciding that she would never be enough, Barbara kept going. The outcome was that she was able to make the world a brighter place and was even able to help people who were worse off than her. This was all possible, not because of her immense skill, but her unbreakable will!

Talent is Hardwired Biologically

What is it that helps these people with zero talent and one hundred percent determination excel? The answer is in their neurons, and it's called myelin. Myelin sheath is the fatty substance that surrounds and coats neurons, and it's also the stuff that helps neurons to send fast impulses to muscles and your extremities. Every time an athlete, a

---

[8]   Hooton, Amanda. "Can Barbara Arrowsmith-Young's Cognitive Exercises Change Your Brain?" *The Sydney Morning Herald*, The Sydney Morning Herald, 21 Apr. 2017, www.smh.com.au/lifestyle/can-barbara-arrowsmithyoungs-cognitive-exercises-change-your-brain-20170419-gvnsn5.html.

surgeon, or a really smart chess player needs to make a creative move—they rely on their myelin to do so.

Each time you make a specific motion, like an artist practicing drawing a straight line—your neurons are sending impulses to your brain—these are carried along their natural pathway by your nerve fibers, which are coated in myelin. Myelin helps by perfecting these nerve signals. For example, you've probably heard about *neuroplasticity*, which means that *neurons that fire together, wire together.* This is referencing myelin and the ability for our brains to light up like Christmas trees, each time we make a specific motion, or think about a specific thought.

If you are really good at typing fast for example, it's probably because you practice a lot—which means your myelin coated nerve fibers send a lot of impulses to your brain. Additionally, if you have a lot of myelin it's because you are practicing very specific, highly trained actions. If you aren't very skilled at something, or you make frequent mistakes during practice, you are practicing those improper nerve firings. So how does this tie in with the rest of this chapter?

Having Skill means having the Will to focus and practice in order to get there. Not everyone is born with natural genetics, some of us (myself included) have to work really hard to get where we want to go in life. If you don't like what you were given at birth, you can work on proper practice in order to get really good muscle memory. Perfect practice, and great form will go a long way towards helping you improve your skills.

Affirmations for Will and Skill:

Embracing the "Whatever It Takes" Mindset

In order to keep yourself focused on your goal, you have to keep your mind programmed to remember that you have what it takes.

Throughout our daily lives, we get so caught up in stress, fear, and anxiety that we forget how good it feels to believe in ourselves!

Use the following affirmations to remind yourself that anything is possible. Saying them to yourself is a great way to make them become a habit. The more you say them, the more you will remember them. But don't just say these words and move on—think back to the stories I shared in this chapter. It will make anything you're going through feel more doable!

- I'm willing to do whatever it takes to be positive.
- I'm willing to do whatever it takes to live with purpose.
- I'm willing to do whatever it takes to be happy.
- I'm willing to do whatever it takes to be a student of life no matter what.
- I'm willing to learn new skills and be the old dog, learning new tricks.

CHAPTER 6:
THE CONSCIOUS OUTLAW

Apple knew who their audience was from the beginning. All successful businesses create a culture around themselves. Because without culture we have nothing. Each of Apple's decisions was strategic, and were aligned with their values, because they knew that the culture they created for their products was surrounded by actual people, who shared those same exact values.

When I was lying in my hospital bed with a burst appendix, I began thinking about values. I only had a 50/50 chance of making it out of surgery. With ulcerative colitis, the surgeon told me the chances of me keeping my colon were slim to none. As I was lying on the bed before I went under, I started to really think about my life and what I have been through. I have always lived my life to the fullest and gone after my dreams. I can honestly say that I don't regret any of the mistakes that I've made as they were great learning experiences. But it made me think about how short life can be. Time is so precise, and yet we waste so much of it. It made me think about how I wanted to be remembered and I started asking myself difficult questions. *Have I been authentic? What do I want people to say about me if I die? Will they say that now?*

I realized that I have been going after my dreams for me and not being truly authentic and following my purpose. Sometimes, I have allowed my ego to take control and put inconsequential things first. Reality really hit me, and I decided to make a pact to myself. If I get out of the surgery, I want to do three things.

1. Inspire
2. Motivate
3. Educate

Luckily, I came out of surgery, but it was a long recovery and I decided it was time to change certain things in my life. I took a teaching job in a lockdown facility helping kids under eighteen, dealing with behavioral problems in order to be of service. I committed to reading a minimum of two books a week to commit to learning. And I also created a creed to live by based on the concepts of the conscious outlaw. All of these were steps towards acting on my values.

The Stoics

"The universe is change; our life is what our thoughts make it."--Marcus Aurelius

"True happiness is... to enjoy the present, without anxious dependence upon the future."-Seneca

"An unexamined life is not worth living."-Socrates

Conscious Outlaws practice the philosophies of the great Stoic leaders by carrying on their practice of emotional intelligence. Marcus Aurelius, Seneca, and Socrates are just a few of the most famous stoic minds who made a massive impact on history. Emotional intelligence, which I will speak about more in the next chapter, involves being conscious of what we think and how we fee. It also illuminates the reasons behind the choices we make. Happiness comes from being grateful and being grateful comes from getting out of fear. When we are grateful we are humble. When we are humble, we remember that life is short, and nothing lasts forever.

Why are Principles and Values Important?

We all have different values and beliefs. For every person on Earth, there is a different 100% complex and unique belief system. In order to get to where we want to be in life, we must learn to conquer our own beliefs. Being able to change our minds means that we must become conscious first. Without consciousness, there is no way for us to understand the reasons behind our actions. However, most of the world is very unconscious of what they are doing, or why they are doing it. Before we can understand and uncover the reasons behind what we are doing today in our lives, we need to go back to the source of where our belief sets are formulated: childhood.

What we experience in our early years becomes part of who we are. These experiences shape what we feel and how we act, whether we like it or not. There's not much that we can do to control these influences. Unfortunately, at least for the first portion of our lives, we are stuck with the perspectives and insights they teach us. So much of who we ultimately become has to do with the way our parents and relatives set the tone of what we value and believe in our early years. These experiences shape the person that we initially become, much of which is beyond our control.

For instance, if growing up your father and mother speak to each other in a loving manner, it is highly likely that you will reciprocate this in your future relationships. On the contrary, if your dad has little awareness of his tone and is violent and abusive and comes home drinking, screaming, and yelling at your mother it will affect the type of person you grow up to be. Most of the time, our family isn't aware of how their actions impact us as children. If our parents are racist, judgmental, pessimistic, shame-based, dysfunctional lunatics there's a good chance we may become the same thing. We only know what we see in the early years from our role models. We don't have the ability to challenge their belief systems because we have limited information and our maps of reality are only charted to the previous destinations where are parents have taken us and what we experience.

The first three years of a child's life is the most important for their learning. These years set the stage for how we will develop once we enter into formal education. Now we are around others who come from completely different environments and have been taught different values. These values begin to influence and shape us, but not nearly as much as our parents, since we've been exposed to those beliefs the most. When our values are challenged in school, we begin to experience problems. This is the reason that so many adolescents get into trouble. What they are told by their parents, teachers, and their icons in the world, are all in conflict. Hormones surge through their bodies, and they never know exactly what to believe.

Parents aren't the only problem shaping our beliefs. Sometimes, it's also the fear of abandonment that can surface in a mix of ways. If we were abandoned by our biological parents, then we have another level of pain to deal with. Without a solid foundation of beliefs in place, we are easily influenced. Without parents that model integrity and solid values and principles where can we learn them, we are left to fend for ourselves.

Another factor that leads us to respond to certain situations is stress. This is especially true if we have a rough childhood or come from poor parenting. When we are under constant stress, our dopamine levels become drained, so we look for any reward to make us feel good. Unfortunately, we look for easy was to get pleasure when we are under stress. But we can spike our dopamine levels in positive ways. Growing up, I lived in fight or flight mode. My early experiences with alcohol led to other drugs, and they led me to my drug of choice: cocaine.

Cocaine made me invincible and tore my life apart. Once I got sober I realized through meditation and exercise that I could get the same effect as I did with drugs and alcohol. However, it was a long road to recovery. What most people don't realize is that we all have vices: sex, gambling, eating, shopping, porn, and video games to name just a few. We need to become aware of what we value and why we value it. Our values shape the decisions we make, and sometimes they are very unconscious. Instead, we must create strong principles based on our values, and live based on those higher needs, rather than the callings of a dopamine craze. It's never too late to find our authentic selves, but to do that, we need to create a value system.

I don't consider myself to be a monk, a saint, or an angel. In fact, I was a pretty good fighter to tell you the truth. However, what I've learned through years of martial arts practice is that nothing is as important as learning *how to avoid a fight*. The deeper work doesn't just involve being able to kick someone's ass, it also means knowing when to use this practice—which is very rarely, if ever. We all must be able to fend for ourselves, and more importantly, stand up for injustice. However, we must also remain conscious. In order to remain conscious, we must rise above the ways of the world, and live life by our own rules. Socrates was an outlaw. He was persecuted and died a criminal's death for "corrupting" the morals of the youth, despite being one of the wisest men in antiquity. Martin Luther King Jr. was jailed several times in his pursuit of equal rights. If we are to learn anything from these *conscious outlaws,* it is this: we must maintain our composure in the face of adversity and take matters into our own hands in order to do the right thing.

When you take matters into your own hands, only you are responsible for the outcome of your life. You are the victor and you can decide to dare to be someone better than you ever imagined. But first, you must distance yourself from the ways of the world. Some may think of you as an *outcast, outlaw, or vigilante* but if you are also conscious, you will be able to make a much larger impact!

In order to become a conscious outlaw, you must embody both the **values and the principles of a conscious outlaw first.** Only then can you truly be able to live the life of your dreams.

10 Values of a Conscious Outlaw

1. Accountability: Being responsible for how we act and treat others is a key principle to becoming the person we are meant to be.

2. Authenticity: Being honest, genuine, and real about how we feel. We act as our true selves and don't compromise our integrity to please others when we know what is right. If everyone is being racist, do we join the crowd or stand beside the person being mistreated?

3. Focus: Being able to concentrate on an activity by giving it our full attention.

4. Generosity: Engaging in the practice of being unselfish. Showing compassion to others and going outside ourselves to bring happiness expecting nothing in return.

5. Reliability: Doing what we say we will do. Being honest and showing up in life when people need us.

6. Patience: Having the ability to create a gap been what we feel and how we choose to respond to people when things don't go as we planned.

7. Being of service: To live with real purpose is to be of service to others. We all need money, but money is the effect, not the cause. Our cause should be to be of service, then the effect will be the money we receive for our work.

8. Hard working: Without hard work we get nothing. People that are jealous and envious are only like this because they fear hard work. Hard work always outshines talent.

9. Simplicity: Keeping things simple and in perspective allows us to live within our means. Once we lose the ability to be simple and only take what we need our egos take over. Once we feel more is better we are puppets to the world.

10. Discipline: No one that succeeds in life does it if they are undisciplined. Being disciplined and practicing good habits allows us to grind past people even if they started with more than us. Everything begins and ends with us. The values we believe in and the principles we practice daily create our life.

The 6 Principles of a Conscious Outlaw

1. A Conscious Outlaw is calm, secure, doesn't complain, blame or play the victim.

2. A Conscious Outlaw creates solutions to situations and finds a positive in every negative situation because they have the power to control their thoughts.

3. A Conscious Outlaw is in control of their emotions, feelings and takes full responsibility of their actions. They know that they have the freedom of choice as they know that no one can ever control them.

4. A Conscious Outlaw knows life is not what happens to you but how you choose to react in the present moment.

5. A Conscious Outlaw knows life is about living with purpose and truth no matter what is going on in the world around them.

6. A Conscious Outlaw takes the road less traveled. They don't follow in other people's footsteps they step to the side and create their own path for others to follow them.

The Daily Meditations of the Conscious Outlaw

Words have an effect on what we believe. And the words that a *conscious outlaw* chooses are important. Being able to lean on certain words can help us to create a renewed sense of strength in times of need. The following are daily words, which you can incorporate into your meditations, mantras, prayers, vision boards, or other daily practices. Let the alphabet of life be your daily reminder to commit to the actions and beliefs necessary to become a conscious outlaw.

The 3 A's in Life

ACCEPT, ATTITUDE, ACTION

If we accept the cards we are dealt in life and keep a positive attitude, we will take the right action to succeed.

The 3 B's in Life

Believe, Breathe, Break Free

We must believe in ourselves, breathe when we are overwhelmed and break free of negative thinking to find happiness.

The 3 C's in Life

Committed, Courage, Consistent

Have the courage to be yourself no matter what others say. Be committed to find your life's purpose and be consistent to make your dreams a reality.

The 3 D's in Life

Determined, Dedicated, Decisive

Be determined, dedicated and decisive when you take the road less travelled and never look back.

The 3 E's in Life

Express, Encourage, Energize

Never be afraid to express yourself. Surround yourself with people that encourage and energize you with power and light.

The 3 F's in Life

Faith, Forgive, Fearless

Have faith in the hard times: they won't last forever. Forgive people when they do you wrong. Be fearless when you go after your goals.

The 3 G's in Life

Grateful, Generous, Genuine

Be Grateful for today as you may not have it tomorrow. Be generous in the love you give and be genuine to your fellow brothers and sisters.

The 3 H's in Life

Humble, Honest, Hard Working

A humble, honest, hardworking person will always turn a bad situation into a blessing.

The 3 I's in Life

Inspire, Intuition, Invincible

Inspire people with your actions. Follow your intuition when you feel lost. Know you are invincible as your spirit cannot be touched.

The 3 J's in Life

Joke, Joy, Jump

Sometimes a little joke can bring some joy. Never be afraid to take a risk and jump to take a leap of faith.

The 3 K's in life

Kind, Keen, Knowledge

Be kind as there is too much hate in the world. Be keen to improve who you are day by day. Thirst for knowledge as we can never stop learning.

The 3 L's in Life

Laugh, Learn, Love

Laugh when you are sad. Sometimes you have to fake it till you make it. Learn when you lose.

Love when you hate; life is too short to carry resentments.

The 3 M's in Life

Motivate, Meditate, Master

Motivate yourself to succeed. Meditate to find your peace. Master your mind so you do not become its slave.

The 3 N's in Life

Nourish, Nurture, Nirvana

Nourish yourself with good food. Find a partner to nurture you through life's ups and downs. Nirvana will be close by.

The 3 O's in Life

Optimistic, Open, Overcome

An optimistic mind set will be open to the gifts the universe has to offer and overcome any obstacles along the way.

The 3 P's in Life

Positive, Passionate, Personal Growth

Positive thinking will bring a positive attitude. Being passionate about what you do in life brings personal growth.

The 3 Q's in Life

Quit, Quality, Quantity

Quit racing around trying to people please and consuming things you don't need. Life is about quality, not quantity.

The 3 R's in Life

Reason, Responsibility, Resiliency

Always have a reason to live your dreams out loud. Take responsibility for the choices you make. One good choice will lead to another. Be resilient: nothing comes easy. Never quit before the magic happens.

The 3 S's in Life

Simple, Spontaneous, Shine

Be simple and yet spontaneous, and you will always shine.

The 3 T's in Life

Thankful, Truth, Trusting

Be thankful moment by moment for what you have. Be truthful to what drives you inside. Be trusting that if you do what is right, life will provide what we need to get by.

The 3 U's in Life

Understanding, Unconditional, Unified

Be understanding when people are reaching out for help. Be unconditional with how you love. Be unified as we are all consciously connected.

The 3 V's in Life

Value, Virtue, Victorious

Value every breath you take, it may be your last. Let virtue garnish your thoughts and actions, and you shall be victorious in your pursuit of happiness.

The 3 W's in Life

Wise, Worry, Wealth

Stop worrying about yesterday, it has already said goodbye. Stop wasting your precious energy trying to run other people's lives. Your wealth and volcanic power lies dormant. Release it, spread your wings and fly.

The 3 X's in Life

X-Ray, Xenophobic, Xenophilia

If you could take an x-ray of your chest, would it be brimming with love? There are too many xenophobic people in the world. We must love others who are different from us, through the practice of xenophilia before it's too late.

The 3 Y's in Life

Yes, Young, Yearn

Say *yes* when a door closes on you and the world says *no*. When one door closes another door opens. You are as young as you feel, time has no meaning. Yearn for greatness and it shall be yours.

The 3 Z's in Life

Zeal, Zest, Zip

Go after your dreams with zeal, zest and zip: nobody likes a zombie.

CHAPTER 7:
WILLPOWER, SELF-DISCIPLINE, AND EMOTIONAL INTELLIGENCE

Becoming a conscious outlaw doesn't just happen overnight. Instead it takes time, guts, and determination to get to that level of personal knowledge and inner wisdom. In order to get to that point, you need to have what I like to call the trifecta: willpower, self-discipline, and emotional intelligence. Having each of these traits will make your life easier because you will be resilient enough to face any challenges that arise. Throughout the rest of this chapter we will examine each of these traits in-depth, so that you can find ways to renew your focus and break through the barriers holding you back.

What is Willpower?

So, we all know what willpower is—the basic control one must have to fight impulses and emotions. However, the question that's important for our discussion is: *do you know how to conjure up more of it?* This is especially crucial when talking about ways to overcome fear, obstacles, and anything else that stands in our way.

Willpower also plays a huge part in our everyday life. Lack of willpower can affect our lives massively if we need to understand how to cultivate it. If we don't have willpower, we will never achieve our goals. When we set a goal to achieve something we have to say *yes* to some things and *no* to others. We must be willing to make sacrifices in order to be successful. If you want to be in shape you may have to give up certain eating habits. That takes the willingness to say *no* to junk food and *yes* to healthy alternatives.

In order to know more about what you actually need and what just sounds like a good idea, you need to ask yourself these two basic questions: *what do I want? and why do I want it?*

As we make choices, we must learn that doing one thing means that we must neglect another. Having a solid awareness of what we want helps us focus on the goal, and ignore the pain that accompanies the work we must put in. I hear people all the time looking for the magic pill to get everything that they want in life. Unfortunately, it doesn't exist. If we aren't willing to sacrifice to succeed, then we will never be happy. Tim Ferriss talks about having a "Not-To-Do-List" and this is a good practice for anyone who is looking to become aware of triggers and weaknesses[9]. Ask yourself: *what am I willing to give up in order to achieve what I want?*

Triggers:

When I first stopped drinking I had to open up a night club which was a huge challenge. But I knew what my triggers were and what I had to do to stay clean and sober. My employees knew my situation and were my eyes and ears. I kept myself busy, and I never kept alcohol in my own home. Removing triggers, means making it easier to get results.

Environment:

Take a conscious look at your environment and surroundings. Then, ask yourself: am I setting myself up to fail or succeed? Don't take two

[9]   Ferriss, Timothy. *The 4-Hour Workweek: Escape 9-5, Live Anywhere, and Join the New Rich.* Harmony Books, 2012.

steps forward and one step back. Instead, eliminate distractions and clean up your surroundings. Choose quiet, calm environments where you can be alone and creative. Turn off your social media distractions. Have food close by if you need to snack, and don't get hung up on little things.

Friends and Family:

Unfortunately, friends and family can either be our best supporters or our biggest haters. They can either uplift us or drain us on our way through life. If friends and family are renting space in your head and getting you off track, you need to set boundaries and limit time with them while you are on your journey towards success.

Work:

We all need to work to make money. But we have to be aware of how much our time spent working is affecting us. Working 16-hour days under stressful conditions then coming home to stress and trying to be on top of your goals is an uphill battle.

When I Choose I Lose:

Every time we make a choice to resist a temptation willpower is drained from our willpower tank. The more we use it, the more we lose it. Study willpower instinct. *How can we preserve our willpower?*

Willpower is a muscle, meaning the more you exercise it, the stronger it gets. If you aren't used to using your willpower, you are probably confusing it with something else. Because chances are, you use it on a very regular basis without even realizing it.

Roy Baumeister explains how willpower works. Now, he's not just anyone, he is a PhD and the director of social psychology at Florida

State University. More importantly, he's also one of the pioneers behind behavioral psychology and the man behind much of what we know about how willpower functions. Roy suggests that our willpower "muscle" can get worn out.[10] That's why you are more likely to cheat on your diet later in the day. It's also one of the major reasons why you need to make sure you are getting adequate rest and proper nutrition.

We need to make sure we get enough sleep in order to be able to say *no* to easy distractions. Lack of sleep will drain our will power tank faster than many other things. Exercise regularly, avoid junk foods, add in some meditation or hobbies. Hang out with people who bring you up, to avoid constantly being in fight or flight mode. We need to learn to pace ourselves, reduce our stress, and set ourselves up in an environment that helps us achieve our goals. Where there is a will there is always a way. Keeping grinding and you can shine.

Self-Discipline Builds on Willpower

Once you have willpower, you can begin building up your self-discipline to become your own guru. Self-discipline is the ability to control one's emotions and overcome our weaknesses, impulses, urges and cravings. A self-disciplined person knows how to delay their gratification, focus on the big picture, and grind through to the end no matter how they feel or what they are faced with. This is the biggest impediment to being able to achieve your dreams. If you aren't able to focus and maintain vigilance you won't be able to get the long-term results you are looking for.

Sometimes, we fall into the trap of believing that the best and brightest were born with amazing amounts of talent, and just effortlessly

---

[10]   Baumeister, Roy F., and John Tierney. *Willpower: Rediscovering the Greatest Human Strength.* Penguin Books, 2012.

arrived at superstardom. However, as we uncovered in *Skill and Will*, it's not about skill, as much as it is about will.

Everyone thinks Michael Jordan had it easy. Yet, he didn't even make his high school team. He was humiliated, awkward, and gangly as a player. However, he didn't give up. Instead, he disciplined himself. Before becoming one of the best players in the history of basketball, he had to practice shooting free throws, working on ball-handling skills, and perfecting his Air Jordan. He wasn't magically one of the best players in the world, he had to discipline himself in order to become one. "I have missed more than 9,000 shots in my career," Jordan has said. "I have lost almost 300 games. I have failed over and over and over again in my life. And that is why I succeed."

Arianna Huffington

Arianna Huffington is the founder and president of The Huffington Post. However, she hasn't always been a successful news platform owner. First, she was a writer. When she decided to write her second book it was rejected on thirty-six separate occasions. Her friends laughed when she decided to launch an online magazine. Today that little online magazine is worth an estimated $315 million. "Perseverance is everything. Everybody has failures, but successful people keep on going."-Arianna Huffington

Walt Disney

Walt Disney went bankrupt before becoming the creator of some of the most beloved cartoons in the world. He opened the doors of his first animation company in 1921, but it ultimately failed. He ended up failing several times before actually tasting success. Snow White was a massive success, but it took a lot of convincing to early doubters who felt the movie would be a flop. Today, we remember Disney—not as a failure—but as a celebrated theme park founder, television and movie network producer. He was truly a visionary, because he was self-disciplined enough to believe in his vision when no one else did.

The Benefits of Being Self-Disciplined

Self-disciplined people practice the self-control to stick to a decision they make without getting distracted by outside temptations. They possess the strength to practice certain habits to help them overcome addictions, procrastination and constantly take inventory of their assets and liabilities.

However, these people aren't insane specimens of human beings, they are just conscious enough to follow a plan. With the right plan, nearly anyone can succeed—including you!

By practicing the following habits of self-disciplined people, you can learn to exhibit self-control and become disciplined enough to achieve your goals. It's important to remember that these things take time and will be delayed gratifications rather than instant manifestations. You must learn how to establish a healthy routine, which will help you overcome the usual blocks that most people face in relationship to getting what they want.

12 Habits of Self-Disciplined People

1. **They Have the Ability to Delay Gratification**
   Avoiding the easy route leads to major gains, and more pleasure later. It also helps you to avoid distractions.

2. **They Can Persevere, Persist and Avoid Procrastination**
   Procrastination robs us all of our brilliance, don't depend on putting things off until the last minute—get started right away.

3. **They Have Self-Control**

   Control is different than discipline. The more self-control you have over your own actions, the easier it is to exert effort into a disciplined routine. Without self-control, you can never have self-discipline.

4. **They Set Macro and Micro Goals**

   Goals, big and small, help us to keep things in perspective.

5. **They Practice Meditation**

   Meditation gets the thinking mind quiet long enough to calm the mind and return you to your natural state.

6. **They Exercise Daily**

   Daily exercise is crucial to wellbeing and keeping the Million Dollar Mindset alive.

7. **They are Self Aware**

   They are aware when they make a mistake and they admit it.

8. **They Have the Ability to Bounce back After a Loss or Failure**

   Shying away from failure doesn't do anything productive.

9. **They Prioritize and Plan**

   Prioritizing and planning are crucial steps to getting to your intended destination.

10. **They Cultivate a Flexible Mindset**

    Being open-minded makes it easier to work with others and to see the bigger picture.

11. **They Have a Life Purpose, Mission and Live by Principles**

    Conscious Outlaws must hone their values and live by them, in order to stay in integrity.

12. **They Cultivate and Protect their Willpower**

    Your willpower is your energy, it must be cultivated and used wisely.

Self-disciplined people know that to be successful at any given task, but they also need to acquire certain skills. However, in 2018, most people dread learning new skills. Skill acquisition is difficult. It takes time, failure, work, and more refined, honed, practice. If you aren't learning new skills, you aren't growing.

In order to achieve success, it's important that you commit to your own growth. Remember, no one else but you can determine your potential. You must own your actions and commit to making things happen on a daily basis.

So how can you tell if you are disciplined enough to be successful? You must be aware of the warning signs that you are undisciplined. The following list will give you some clues. Keep in mind, no one is judging you. Taking inventory is part of the process to become a better, saner, more dedicated human being.

10 Traits of an Undisciplined Person.

1. **Lack of Focus**

   A lack of focus manifests in feelings of depression, overwhelm, and distraction.

2. **Procrastination**

   Procrastination is a silent killer of many hopes and dreams. Get started right away, and you'll be less likely to put things off for too long.

3. **Victim Mentality**

   Playing the victim is the easy way out, and it's an easy way to convince yourself to stop working so hard.

4. **Lack of Grit**

   Grit refers to being able to keep your head down and work, if you lack grit, you lack the fortitude to get the job done.

5. **Poor Preparation**

Not preparing well means sacrificing opportunities and self-sabotaging your responsibilities.

6. **Fixed Mindset**

Being closed-minded can make it tougher to see progress.

7. **Fear of Failure**

Fear of failure holds many people back from ever getting started. Fear of not trying is much scarier.

8. **Entitlement**

Thinking that the world owes you something is a sure recipe for failure. Be humble.

9. **Catastrophic Thinking**

Worrying that the sky is falling is another bad habit. Luckily, you can always change your mindset.

10. **Pessimistic Attitude**

Being negative all the time is no way to live. Try adopting a positive attitude for just seven days and see what happens.

If you noticed any of the ten warning signs of lack of discipline and think that you may need to cultivate more discipline start by following these five steps.

1. **Becoming Self Aware of your Bad Habits.**

   Bad habits can be tough to spot, but after a week or so of paying attention, you will begin to see where you are wasting time and energy.

2. **Understand the Consequences of the Choices you Make**

   Every action has consequences, aim to practice Pareto's law, where 20% of your action creates 80% of the results.

3. **Take Responsibility for your Choices**

Own up to the decisions and commitments you have made, which will make it much easier for you to be a person with integrity, authenticity, and drive.

4. **Be Aware When you get off Track**

Everyone makes mistakes. No one is perfect at their diet, or at anything else in life. A mistake to you could seem like a big deal, but it's not. Every scientific discovery came from a mistake!

5. **Set Goals and Stick to them *No Matter What.***

Don't give up on your goals just because they are challenging, keep going and make it work!

Emotional Intelligence and Perception

Our emotions set the tone for how we react and respond in life. The more aware of them we are, the easier it is for us to make smart, responsible choices based on willpower and self-discipline. However, if we aren't aware of what our emotions are saying, or what other the emotions of others are telling us, we will inevitably make choices that aren't right. In order to protect ourselves from falling out of alignment, we must be able to not only manage our willpower and self-discipline, but we must learn to control our emotions. Being emotionally intelligent is challenging, but it can also be very easy.

Once we develop a certain level of emotional intelligence we learn that life is always about us. We are the ones behind our choices, and we are the reason for the consequences in our lives. Learning to work with others and finding solutions that provide a win-win for all parties involved in our life is very important. Domestic violence, school shootings and divorce rates are at an all-time high. Because, many times, we act before we think, we don't always process our emotions.

Once we start to become self-aware of our emotions and practice self-control we start to change our perceptions. We never see things the same as other people. We all have different maps of reality due to what we have experienced and who are parents are and where we grew up. However, having the ability to see things from another point of view can affect the way we live our lives.

For example, early last year, I was a partner in a restaurant in NYC. The place was always packed with a fun upbeat crowd. One night, I was table touching to make sure the guests were getting their needs met when a patron informed me there was a drunk customer annoying some other patrons.

I wandered over slowly to see a gentleman talking belligerently to a couple of ladies. He wasn't a small guy, so I approached him slowly to read the situation. Being in the restaurant and nightlife business for over twenty years, I never move in on people too quickly when they are intoxicated. As I approached, I could see he was really drunk and needed to be cut off. I introduced myself as one of the owners. I didn't get the best response, but I could see that the guy really wasn't a threat, just a little too drunk. We started chatting and he told me he had just been fired and that his wife had left him. I approached him with compassion because now his intoxication made sense. As we kept chatting, I tried my best to walk him out the door and away from the other patrons at the bar he was sitting at. He was holding a briefcase. I asked him what he did for a living, and he said, "let me show you."

He opened up a briefcase and inside was a set of expensive knives. Being in the restaurant business, I knew he was a chef, and not a trained assassin. After about half an hour of sharing stories, I put him in a taxi and off he went. That night on the subway I was reflecting on the event and realized how bad things would have turned out if I wasn't compassionate. The man could have gotten belligerent and used the knives to harm someone in my restaurant. Being in recovery, I naturally have a soft spot for drunks, because I have made an ass of myself many times.

The next day, around noon, I was in the restaurant seating customers when the same man came in. He apologized for his actions the night before. I told him it was no problem and that I was glad he was alright. He offered to buy me lunch, which I gladly accepted. As we sat down I could tell he wanted to share some things. He asked me why I was so nice to him. I explained to him that I was in recovery and that I help addicts get clean and sober. He confided that he was very glad I had spoken so calmly to him, and that it had saved his life. I asked him how? He broke down as he said that night he wanted to kill his boss for firing him. But because I was nice he let it go. I took a breath and realized how one moment of compassion and empathy can make such a huge difference.

Keep in mind, I have acted out many times. As a result, I try to give people a pass when I feel disturbed or someone crosses me. Is it easy? Hell no. But in the end, what are we really fighting over when it all goes down and we die? Land, houses, cars, money—none of it comes with us when we die. We never know where someone is coming from or where they are going so why get caught in the cross hairs? I know when someone cuts me off, to stop and just breathe. When someone has forty items in the ten items or less line, I let it go. When someone posts something negative on one of my posts or blogs, does it really matter in the grand scheme of things? If we can seek to be ten percent more compassionate and show ten percent more empathy every day, imagine what we could do in the world?

I believe in having positive role models that can help us to shape our lives. One of my favorites is a man named Don Ritchie. Don is a fellow Australian. He is responsible for saving the lives of 160 people and counting from suicide attempts at The Gap, which is a huge cliff in Sydney. It is known all over the world as a place where thousands of people go to plunge to their deaths. However, Ritchie was a local resident who lived nearby, who spent more than four decades making a difference and talking people out of killing themselves. He was recently awarded the Medal of the Order of Australia for his service, and has been named as a Hero several times, while receiving numerous medals for his contribution.[11]

So how did he do it? He would offer potential suicide victims, a simple cup of tea and discuss life with them. He didn't have a master's degree in counseling or psychology. Instead, he just shared his kindness and his incredible spirit with them by showing compassion and empathy for another human who feels lost, alone, and confused. A simple smile can change someone's day. We need to be of service if we want the Universe to give us what we need. If we live with self-awareness and social awareness we will realize we don't need to act out in anger or greed. By breathing before we react a lot can change. Not only in our own lives, but in the lives of everyone we come into contact with, as well.

---

[11]   Pearlman, Jonathan. "Australians Mourn Don Ritchie-the Angel of The Gap." *The Telegraph*, Telegraph Media Group, 14 May 2012, www.telegraph.co.uk/news/ worldnews/australiaandthepacific/australia/9264571/Australians-mourn-Don-Ritchie-the-Angel-of-The-Gap.html.

CHAPTER 8: PUTTING IT ALL TOGETHER

Now that we've discussed how our emotional intelligence, willpower, and discipline can be our greatest allies in creating a life we desire, it's important to recap what we've learned in this book.

Cultivating the right daily habits keeps us on point and successful in life, and it's important that each day we actively strive towards doing our best. Remember, progress not perfection. In this book we've covered a lot of ground. From getting out of fear, to learning how to overcome the obstacles that hold us back—it's vital that you cement the tools and strategies in this book in order to be able to call on them, when you need them most. Keep in mind, that when you are struggling you aren't going to want to do this work. So, you have to be vigilant and disciplined to commit to these self-improvement strategies not only when you want to do them, but especially when you really don't want to.

Creating an unbreakable mindset isn't just about reading a self-help book or going to a seminar. We have to implement daily practices that become habits of success to make ourselves unbreakable. Every successful entrepreneur, coach, athlete, CEO or leader practices certain disciplines to become successful and to keep flourishing. If we don't keep sharpening our sword it gets blunt and is useless when it comes to battle time. The exact same concept applies with our mindset work. You have to continue daily maintenance in order to stay in the best shape possible. So here are some tools that you can practice every day to keep you unbreakable.

In Chapter One we talked about managing our fears. Fear is the biggest detriment to most high-achieving people. Without the ability to make fear our friend, we will never be able to reach our full potential.

Tool 1. Practice the Stop Method

The STOP method helps us create a gap between what we feel and how we choose to respond. The STOP method not only helps us manage fear but can help us when we face adversity and need to find a solution to a problem. When our inner critic is giving us a beating, the STOP method allows us to identify our disturbance and move forward. The STOP method will help us stay on track when we feel we aren't sticking to a plan, but instead are getting distracted from our goals. It is the foundational tool that will help us to concur our inner critic and manage our will power, discipline and EQ.

S-Stop
T-Take a breath
O-Observe
P-Proceed.

In Chapter Two we set out to start finding solutions to problems. We realized that we will need to overcome certain things in order to get to where we want to go, and that the journey is all about the six inches between our ears. In order to face adversity, you must have a positive mindset to be able to go above and beyond!

Tool 2: Daily Inventory

Inventory is important because just like with anything worth doing if you don't know what you have, and what you still need to get, you won't be able to make the best choices. You have to take inventory to be successful. Practice the following inventory daily.

Try breaking it down like this.

1. How is my attitude this morning? Starting our day with the right attitude is paramount to being successful.
2. What do I need to accept in my life today?
3. What actions do I need to take to be successful and turn my dreams into a reality?
4. What can I be grateful about?

In Chapter Three we discussed how to turn our dreams into a reality. I showed you how I was able to do that, and gave you some realistic timelines of just how long and difficult the journey to success will be. It won't be easy but knowing how long it will take you to achieve and reach your goals is vital. Then, breaking it down into bite-size, manageable pieces is the pathway to success.

If you haven't already, complete this simple exercise. It could change the trajectory of your life!

WHAT IS YOUR 10-YEAR GOAL?

WHAT IS YOUR 5-YEAR GOAL?

WHAT IS YOUR 1-YEAR GOAL?

WHAT ARE YOUR MONTHLY GOALS?

WHAT ARE YOUR WEEKLY GOALS?

WHAT ARE YOUR DAILY GOALS?

In Chapter Four we worked on concurring our inner critic. Inner critics can be our biggest saboteur, or they can propel us towards a more powerful track.

Tool 4. Motivation Reality Check

One of the biggest problems that the inner critic will cause in your life is that he or she will cause you to procrastinate. So, in order to stop that I want you to do a little conscious change exercise with me.

First write down on a piece of paper how old you are. Then, write the number eighty above it. Now, subtract the two numbers. Write that number on a separate piece of paper, index card, or business card and keep it in your purse or wallet for ninety days. Whenever you begin to procrastinate I want you to catch yourself and pull out that number. That's how many more summers you have left on this Earth. Are you using them, or wasting them?

In Chapter Five we discussed how skill is great but will is even better. We discussed some famous examples of people without much talent, doing extraordinary things. No matter where you are at in life, you can accomplish the impossible by being committed to putting in the hard work.

Tool 5 Find a Hobby and Be of Service.

All work no play makes life a drag. Finding a hobby with a group of people we like can only improve our quality of life. Being of service in a group helps build our oxytocin as well as dopamine and serotonin.

Be Committed: Once a month try and be of service within your chosen charity or service group.

Chapter Six stressed the importance of having principles and a creed to live by. I shared with you my creed of the Conscious Outlaw and explained how we must be devoted to ideals bigger than ourselves in order to hold ourselves accountable and make the most of our lives.

Tool 6. Friends and Family

Set aside time for close friends and family. I can admit this has been the hardest thing for me to do. Always being on the grind trying to chase our dreams can give us tunnel vision. We have to get in the practice of putting aside quality time for friends and family. Remember life is short, and we only have so many summers to enjoy.

Last but not least, in Chapter Seven we learned how to manage our willpower, cultivate discipline, and use our emotional intelligence. All three of these skills are sequential and the more we improve one, the more we learn how to harness the others.

Tool 7. Start Reading More and Use Social Media Less

There's an old adage that rings true for most of us in our digitally addicted culture: *leaders are readers*. Just like daily exercise, we need to work our memory and mind, or we start to forget things. I have now started to read a minimum of one book per week, and it has absolutely improved many aspects of my life. I've noticed benefits such as improved memory, concentration, and refined focus and my life has been greatly enhanced by this simple decision.

Being dyslexic is quite a challenge. A guy like me, who reads slow, reads about 20 lines a minute. With most lines averaging about 10 words per line, that is equivalent to 200 hundred words. If I read 30 minutes in the morning and 30 minutes at night I'm hitting 12,000 words a day. If I read seven days in a week, that's 72,000 words a week.

The average 250 to 300-page books averages between 60k to 70,000 words. So that's a book a week. Turning off social media notifications will help you control that quick fix dopamine hit you have gotten used to receiving. I try to only get my email a couple of times a day and only go on social media every now and then to post. I used to waste so much time looking through dumb pages and it got me nowhere. Be vigilant, be disciplined, and use your free time to learn rather than to skim through cat photos and your friend's over-priced lunches. In a year, you'll be glad you read 52 more books, instead of getting an extra few hundred likes on social media.

If you've read to this point, then I have to applaud you for your ability to follow through and commit. It is my sincerest wish that you will use the ideas, concepts, tools, and stories in this book to influence you on your life journey. The path ahead won't be easy, but always remember that there are millions of other people who are striving towards their goals just like you.

I encourage you to take some of Ferriss Bueller's sage advice and stop for a moment to take a look around. Nothing here lasts forever. Life is short, and we only get one go around. From this moment on you have an opportunity to take the road less traveled and be the star of your own movie. Write your script and play your role. Keep failing until you shine. I'm living proof that if you stand in line long enough, you eventually get to the front. Keep chasing y

our dreams no matter what people say. It's your life to live! Choose to be a Conscious Outlaw!

Printed and bound by PG in the USA

USA2018PGIL